ALL TRUMPED UP

Our Lionhearted President

George E. Smock
(Brother Jed)

The Campus Ministry USA

Terre Haute IN

Dedication

To my grandfathers, James C. Smock (1861-1926) and Frederick T. Gelder (1874-1955), both of whom were long time Republican officeholders, Christian gentlemen, community leaders and faithful family men.

Acknowledgments

--Thank you Pastor David Coke for formatting my Facebook posts.
--Mario Bertoluzzi and Bro Cope, proofreaders
--Cindy Smock, editor
--Paul Temple, cover artist

TABLE OF CONTENTS

Foreword...7

Author's Preface.....................................11

Introduction...15

Chapter I: The Primaries.....................23

Chapter II: General Election................69

Chapter III: President Elect................117

Chapter IV: The Inauguration............135

Chapter V: First 100 Days..................153

Appendix A: Literally but not Seriously..197

Appendix B: Frederich T. Gelder.........205

Foreword
By Pastor David Coke

Greatness has been understated in our modern culture. The reasons are multifaceted but they stem from the loss of REALITY. This loss has occurred first, from gross and total self-aggrandizement (everyone thinks of themselves as grand or great, thus making greatness equal sameness, the great socialist lie). Second, from the loss of inductive thinking, that process of predicting the future based on the past (the reality of the past has been ignored or redefined, thus making the future terrifying rather than promising). Third, from the replacement of substance with symbolism (the idea that if I say it, feel it, or display it, then I have accomplished it; thus, rendering action irrelevant).

Greatness can only be recognized in the context of reality; the comprehension of things as they are, not what we imagine them to be. Donald Trump is a great leader precisely because he lives realistically and has no connection with the modern fantasy world. He is grounded firmly in the reality of who he is, what he has accomplished and what he will do.

All great leaders also speak a common "language." It is not the new language, the language of sports, the "hood," social media and millennials; it is the language of the past, the language of TRUTH. Sadly, this language has become extinct in modern leadership and been replaced with the language of religious and political correctness.

Donald Trump speaks the language of truth fluently: pronouncing, repeating, pausing, and inflecting, in perfect diction, those words and phrases which describe REALITY. The "dictionary" of this language is the Bible, the Declaration of Independence, the Constitution of the United States of America and the lives of those men and women who gave themselves for its preservation. All great leaders have the same things in common, they are loved by a few, hated by the many, exonerated by history and most importantly, they say and DO THE RIGHT THINGS.

The content of this book is a compilation of the thoughts of Rev. George Smock, aka, Brother Jed, posted on his Facebook page regarding "The Donald," President Donald J. Trump. As you will quickly realize, Bro. Jed was a supporter of Mr. Trump early in his campaign. For this support, Bro. Jed endured ridicule, mockery, hatred, and ostracism by many of his "friends," similar to the treatment Mr. Trump endured by his "friends." These indecencies are common treatments suffered and endured by great leaders. Those who know Bro. Jed well, also know that he experiences this treatment by his audience for 5 hours a day as he preaches the gospel of Jesus Christ on the college campus, so the desired affect was like "water off a duck's back," Great leaders always overcome opposition for their "cause is just."

In terms of leadership, there are many similarities between the campaign and embattled presidency of Donald J. Trump and the ministry and mission of Rev. George Smock. I met Bro. Jed and Sister Cindy in 1984 when he came to my home town, Dixon, IL, for a Saturday night meeting in the Loveland Community Building, hosted by my mother and Harry and Joyce Quick. I was impressed with the boldness and purity of this couple and their willingness to be mocked, considered fools and rejected even by loved ones, to fulfill the great commission. *"And He said to them, 'Go into all the world and preach the gospel to all creation'"* (Mark 16:15). For me, they were the first Christians to speak of confrontational evangelism as opposed to friendship evangelism, which had become silent evangelism, i.e. don't say anything, let's just be friends. (It could be called, Mr. Rogers evangelism.)

I have observed Jed and Cindy in our home, on the campus and at conferences for these many years, and I have never been disappointed in them or had reason to question their wisdom, commitment and courage. I consider Bro. Jed a great leader and a great man.

George Smock is a highly-educated man, who could have taught at the university level, but upon his conversion, left all, took up his cross (sacrificed his plans) and went into the highways and byways to compel sinners to come in. Jed Smock has, for over forty years, preached to college and university students the Biblical call to repent, make restitution and save themselves from sin to a life of holiness by faith in Jesus Christ. This message has been met with violence, argument, heckling and disbelief from the students and returned with plain speaking, patience, peace, wit, and profound truth from Brother and Sister Smock.

Donald Trump is a great leader and like the King of Nineveh who called his kingdom to repentance from their sin to SAVE their lives, President Trump is calling for a national repentance from the sin of government waste, corruption and destruction of our freedoms to save the life of our nation.

Jonah warned Nineveh that God would destroy them in 40 days, and Mr. Trump believed that liberalism would destroy this country in four more years of democratic rule. He responded by running for the Presidency, sacrificing his privacy, his past and his businesses, enduring the most outrageous lies and innuendos to be elected, viz. covering himself with sack cloth and ashes, and is calling every citizen, every jack ass, every elected official into account.

The Apostle Paul, a Roman Citizen, who was at times imprisoned and finally executed by his government writes, *"First of all, then, I urge that entreaties and prayers, petitions and thanksgivings, be made on behalf of all men, for kings and all who are in authority, so that we may lead a tranquil and quiet life in all godliness and dignity. This is good and acceptable in the sight of God our Savior, who desires all men to be saved and to come to the knowledge of the truth,"* (1Ti 2:1-4).

PREFACE

All Trumped Up is the story of how I purchased my ticket, boarded the Trump train and rode it to victory.

By training, I am a historian and taught United States history at the college level before becoming a college campus evangelist in 1972. I have been an avid watcher of the political scene since Eisenhower's first campaign in 1951. Except for a brief interlude during the late sixties, I have been a lifelong Republican from a strong Republican family on both my parents' sides.

Before Donald J. Trump officially announced his candidacy, I gave him little attention. He seemed to be a braggart who probably had a lot less money than he claimed. It was unbecoming for a man of great means to flaunt his wealth. He was just another rich liberal, who had over the years spoken favorably of Democrats and liberal causes. I had never watched an episode of *"The Apprentice."* From the beginning, the Republicans had a good line-up from which to pick a candidate and we could easily support any of them against Hillary; Trump was in my mind the least likely to gain the nomination.

However, the news reports of his candidacy and his politically incorrect statements against illegal aliens from Mexico caught my attention. His frontal attacks on the media and his media savvy further captured my notice. The Great Wall of Trump and making Mexico pay for it seized my imagination. Could this billionaire businessman actually be a viable candidate?

Trump used the confrontational tactics of open-air preachers, such as the name calling, "Low Energy Jeb," "Little Marco," and "Lyin' Ted." Trump had an engaging and creative sense of humor, which made politics fun. What is this guy going to say next? Who could not be impressed with the numbers and enthusiasm he gathered at his public rallies? He quickly dominated the Republican debates. Certainly, no candidate could come close to his skill in connecting with the people.

This book is a compilation of my Facebook statuses and notes on Trump. Written in a FB style; my posts begin over two months after he announced his candidacy. Even after I began to like Trump, I hesitated to publicly talk positively of him out of concern of offending friends. How could a Christian minister, knowing of Trump's two divorces, reputation as a womanizer, past supporter of liberal politics, and his casino enterprises, possibly endorse such a "sinner" for President?

On the other hand, it was impressive that he did not smoke, drink and take drugs. Heavy drinking has been the downfall of many politicians. Also, he spoke more boldly in support of Christianity than any other candidate. The more he angered the liberals, the media and the Republican Party establishment, the more I was drawn to him. Plus, Christian leaders, whom I respected and who were active in politics, were beginning to endorse Trump.

By the fall semester of 2015, I began to speak of Trump positively in my open-air meetings on college campuses and sometimes quoted him in order to provoke dialogue. Eventually, I started introducing my preaching team as, "Evangelicals for Donald J. Trump." Initially, this was partially to get the goat of liberal students. A few students on each campus confided in me that they were Trump supporters, when most students were enamored with Bernie Sanders, the Socialist. The college girls, even the strong feminists, seemed to have little interest in Hillary Clinton.

The more I spoke and wrote statuses concerning Trump, the more enthusiastic I became for his candidacy. The more opposition that came to me, especially from the "Never Trumpers," the more supportive I grew.

Reader, it is not too late to get on the Wabash Cannonball with Engineer Trump and his fireman, the Hoosier, Mike Pence:

*From the great Atlantic Ocean to the wide Pacific shore
She climbs flowery mountain, o'r hills and by the shore
She's mighty tall and handsome,
And she's known quite well by all
You can set your watch to - the Wabash Cannonball.*

*Oh, listen to the jingle, the rumble and the roar
As she glides along the woodland,
o'r hills and by the shore
She climbs the flowery mountain,
Hear the lonesome hobos call
She glides along the woodland, the Wabash Cannonball.*

INTRODUCTION: TWO GREAT MEN OF HISTORY

By Jed Smock

Scottish philosopher, Thomas Carlyle (1795-1881), stated, *"The history of the world is but the biography of great men."* The *great man theory* is God's philosophy of history, since the Bible records the biographies of heroic men.

Adam's wrong choice to succumb to temptation brought sin into the world and the Second Adam, Jesus Christ, by refusing temptation, brought redemption to mankind. Between the first man and the God-man many protagonists arise to carry out God's plan of redemption and many antagonists emerge to oppose God's strategy.

In the book of Genesis we read of Jacob, one of the eminent men in Biblical history, who was a twin son of Isaac and Rebekah. God raised up this patriarch to bring salvation to the world. The other twin, Esau, was the first born but when Jacob came out of his mother's womb, he grabbed Esau by his heal, which is the beginning of a great struggle between the brothers.

The boys grew up. Esau was a sportsman and hunter, the favorite of his father. Jacob was upright and single-minded, the pet of his mother. One day when Esau came home from the hunt, faint and hungry, he asked Jacob to feed him a bowl of lentils. Jacob was an ambitious man who grasped *The Art of the Deal.* He caught Esau in a weak moment and demanded that he sell his birthright. The carnal, fleshly Esau despised his birthright and sold it to Jacob for a meal.

Like Jacob, Donald J. Trump appreciates the importance of Americans' birthrights, among which are life, liberty and the pursuit of happiness. Trump is a man who pursued happiness and obtained the American Dream, which the Democrats, who have the spirit of Esau, despise. They want to make America like Europe and have no respect for American Exceptionalism. As Jacob was determined to get the rights of the first-born son, Mr. Trump is dedicated to regaining American birthrights, which are vanishing on account of Democrat policies.

Later, when the twins' father, Isaac, is old and his eyes dim, Jacob, through deception, gets his father to confirm the birthright by bestowing his blessing of the first-born son on Jacob instead of Esau. Jacob will allow no one, not even his father, to override the foolish deal, which Esau made.

From the beginning of his campaign, Mr. Trump ridiculed the "stupid" American negotiators of trade deals, especially with China, Mexico and Iran. Mr. Trump touts himself as the master negotiator. He has the spirit of Jacob.

Instead of acknowledging his own foolishness, Esau hates Jacob and is determined to kill the "Supplanter." Rebekah encourages Jacob to flee for his life to her brother Laban's home in Haran. She convinces her husband Isaac to send Jacob to Laban to take one of his daughters for a wife. In Jacob's journey, he stopped at a certain place and laid his head upon stones for a pillow:

"He dreamed, and behold a ladder set up on the earth, and the top of it reached to heaven: and behold the angels of God ascending and descending on it. And, behold, the Lord stood above it, and said, I am the Lord God of Abraham thy father, and the God of Isaac: the land whereon thou liest, to thee will I give it, and to thy seed; And thy seed shall be as the dust of the earth, and thou shalt spread abroad to the west, and to the east, and to the north, and to the south: and in thee and in thy seed shall all the families of the earth be blessed. And, behold, I am with thee, and will keep thee in all places whither thou goest, and will bring thee again into this land; for I will not leave thee, until I have done that which I have spoken to thee of"—Genesis 28:12-15.

Godly men had been dreaming of a Trump presidential bid for years. In 2011, a group of ministers with a prophetic anointing led by long-time Trump friend, Paula White, laid hands upon Trump and prayed for God's guidance on his candidacy for President. Sometime later, Trump concluded the timing was not right.

However, four years following, on June 16, 2015, with great fanfare, Donald J. Trump and his lovely wife, Melania, descend the escalator of the Trump Tower to announce his candidacy for the Republican nomination for president of the United States. The 58-story skyscraper at the time of its completion in 1983 was the tallest structure of its type in the city of New York and remains among the highest buildings in the city.

It was as if the Trump Tower and its escalator connected heaven and earth! Trump descended the escalator and God started the process to ascend him to the Presidency of the United States and *"leader of the free world!"*

Prophecies soon revealed to Christian leaders that Trump was God's man to become the 45th President of the United States. Leading evangelicals, such as Jerry Falwell, Jr., quickly boarded the Trump train bound for the White House.

Despite some setbacks in Haran, through shrewd dealing with his Uncle Laban over a 20-year period, Jacob leaves with his wives and eleven sons who were destined to lead great tribes of Hebrew peoples. His beloved son, Joseph, was to in effect rule Egypt. Indeed, Jacob had *"increased exceedingly"* in his exile.

Trump was born into wealth gained by his father, Fred, in the real estate business. Upon college graduation, Donald received a one-million dollar loan from his father, which in Manhattan real estate is not that much money. Through *"The Art of the Deal,"* Donald expanded his family fortune from millions into billions of dollars. Meanwhile, despite two divorces, he raised successful sons and daughters, who became great assets in his run for the presidency.

When Jacob neared the country of Esau, he sent presents before him of large herds of livestock to appease the possible anger and hatred that Esau may still have had for Jacob. Jacob was not overly trusting of his estranged brother. Jacob knew that part of the peace process would be costly. He understood a proverb which Solomon later penned, *"A man's gift maketh room for him, and bringeth him before great men"*—Proverbs

18:16. And another, *"A gift in secret pacifieth anger: and a reward in the bosom strong wrath"—Proverbs 21:14.*

Many Republicans, not appreciating such proverbs, were critical of Trump since he had been a long-time contributor to Democrat politicians, policies and programs. But those of us in the know understand that such gifts were the price of doing business and making deals in the high level of commercial affairs in which Trump negotiated.

As Jacob waited to hear from Esau, he was alone at night; Jacob wrestled with a mysterious man all night, who threw his thigh out of joint in the fight. Still Jacob, ever the negotiator, would not let him go in the morning despite the man's demands:

> *"He said, 'Let me go, for the day breaketh.' And he said, 'I will not let thee go, except thou bless me.' And he said unto him, 'What is thy name?' And he said, 'Jacob.' And he said, 'Thy name shall be called no more Jacob, but Israel: for as a prince hast thou power with God and with men, and hast prevailed.' And Jacob asked him, and said, 'Tell me, I pray thee, thy name.' And he said, 'Wherefore is it that thou dost ask after my name?' And he blessed him there. And Jacob called the name of the place Peniel: 'for I have seen God face to face, and my life is preserved'"-- Gen 32:26-30.*

Afterwards, Esau greeted and received Jacob and his family warmly. Jacob was able to negotiate an acceptable peace with his brother and their long struggle subsided.

Jacob, the *"Supplanter,"* became Israel, the Prince, who prevailed in a wrestling match with God Almighty; he received the promises and blessings initially given to his grandfather, Abraham, *"that in thy seed all the nations of the earth will be blessed."* Through all of Jacob's trials, he grew stronger in spirit and he was one of the main instruments to make the small country of Israel the greatest nation of the ancient world. Israel was magnificent because it represented God to the nations of the earth.

Our pilgrim fathers considered America to be the new Israel. A nation destined to bring blessing to the world and an example of freedom, self-reliance and opportunity. In contrast, Democrats see America as the cause of the world's problems. Domestically, they promote economic dependence on government, which is the Welfare State.

Jacob was a winner; Trump said, *"We need a government that is committed to winning and has experience in winning. I'm a practical businessman who has learned that when you believe in something, you never stop, you never quit, and if you get knocked down, you climb right back up and keep fighting until you win. That's been my strategy all my life, and I've been very successful following it."*

Jacob was able to win in his struggles with Esau and even prevail in a wrestling match with God. Trump won the presidency against all of the predictions of the pundits, the plots of the Democrats and the lies of the hostile media. In the first few months of his presidency we have seen more action coming from the White House than we had in decades. Over the next four years, we shall see President Trump complete his victory by implementing his strategies to Make America Great Again.

"We need somebody who can take the brand of the United States and make it great again. Ladies and gentlemen: I am officially running for president of the United States, and we are going to make our country great again,"
Donald J. Trump, Campaign kickoff, June 16, 2015.

Chapter 1

The Primaries

"I would build a great wall, and nobody builds walls better than me. Believe me. And I'll build it very inexpensively. I'll build a great, great wall on our southern border and I will have Mexico pay for that wall. Mark my words."

Gutter Clean

Wednesday, August 26, 2015 at 10:42pm EDT

Perhaps the most appealing trait of Mr. Trump is the manner in which he stands up to the media jackals, unlike anyone in my lifetime of watching American politics. The only one that would even come close to Trump was Spiro Agnew. Trump has more charm and spontaneity than Nixon's VP.

The Fourth Estate has intimidated the Republicans for decades; it is refreshing to watch the boldness and humor with which the Donald handles the likes of the Mexican Judge and the foxy lady (Megyn). The jackals can't stop him because they need Trump to boost their ratings. Everyone is tuning in to hear what the man has to say next. Usually, it is common sense stuff. Most Americans are not policy wonks nor do they have a definable political philosophy, whether from the left or the right. Trump is a pragmatist, who actually believes he can "Make America Great Again." Daily, he seems to be convincing more and more of the electorate that he has the skills, commitment and optimism to do that very thing.

Monday, August 31, 2015 at 8:15pm EDT

What do my FB friends think of Dr. Michael Brown's letter asking Trump to change his approach? Personally, I find it to be weak and it demonstrates a misunderstanding of the Trumpster. He is not shooting himself in the foot. He is taking good shots at media personalities, Hillary, Obama and Jeb. Much of politics has always been in the gutter. Trump gets into the gutter and so far comes out cleaner every time.

Norman Vincent Peale knew how to connect with people. Seems like Trump learned something from Peale. I am afraid Brown would not fare too well in a street ministry, although I don't know much about him. I think Trump would understand open-air evangelism, when sometimes we "get down and dirty."

Thursday, September 10, 2015 at 9:37am EDT

I must confess my first impression of Carly Fiorina was that she was not photogenic and that she needed a makeover especially concerning her hair. But then I prefer the Kim Davis look over the Carly and Hillary fashion. The Trumpster makes me laugh.

Monday, September 14, 2015 at 7:08pm EDT

As usual Rush Limbaugh understands the Trump phenomenon when no one else does.

Tuesday, September 15, 2015 at 9:34pm EDT

Megyn Kelly asks Carly F., "Doesn't it matter if Donald Trump is a sexist?" Who cares whether he is a sexist or not? That is a liberal concern. Of course, I am not sure what a sexist is. I have been accused of being one. They say Trump is not a conservative. Is Megyn a conservative?

Wednesday, September 16, 2015 at 8:37pm EDT

We need a man who has his finger on the nuclear button who is not afraid to press it if the situation demands it. I think Trump has the temperament to do so.

Tuesday, September 29, 2015 at 8:56pm EDT
Coach Bobby Knight has endorsed Donald Trump.

Wednesday, October 7, 2015 at 10:34pm EDT
Dr. Ben Carson is right on the Oregon shooting: *"I would not just stand there and let him shoot me,"* Carson said. *"I would say 'Hey, guys, everybody attack him! He may shoot me but he can't get us all."*
I have said this after all the mass shootings. Why should he be criticized for saying the obvious? I am glad Trump is backing up his rival on this. Could we have a Trump/Carson ticket?

Friday, October 9, 2015 at 11:24am EDT
The Trumpster is something else; I know there is no substance in this clip; however, this Hispanic woman is priceless for promoting Trumpism. Trump knows how to connect with people unlike anyone else and in the end this will gain him much support.

Friday, November 27, 2015 at 10:55pm EST
No wonder Trump wasn't all that impressed with McCain who opposed waterboarding. There shouldn't be any question about it. We have too many hand wringing conservatives. Waterboarding is really too humane for these Muslim cutthroats.

Monday, November 30, 2015 at 9:02pm EST
"The Making of Donald Trump" now playing on the History Channel. I am watching.

Saturday, December 5, 2015 at 11:04am EST

A Trump rally is much like a campus preach. These vermin who interrupt Trump are just playing into his hands. The conflict makes his campaign more exciting. Trump handles himself well, smiling and occasionally making a comment, all the time showing his disgust.

Sometimes it gets to the point on campus, that all we can do is stand our ground. That's all we have to do. Students will soon confirm everything we have been saying about their depravity. Of course, a big apparent difference is that the majority of the crowd is on the Donald's side. I say apparent because there are more (the Heavenly host) that be with us, than be with our opponents and detractors on campus.

Wednesday, December 16, 2015 at 6:49pm EST

All this talk I hear from the media and politicians about how fearful the electorate is over our safety disturbs me. We heard a lot about it on the debates last night. We are Americans! We should not fear anyone, especially the wicked Muslims. They ought to fear us! At least Trump talks tough, which is the reason he is doing well in the polls. When men fear God, they fear not man.

Thursday, December 17, 2015 at 11:03pm EST

Trump has a stage presence that none of the other candidates can come close to matching. The Donald has appeal to virtually all demographics. He would make mincemeat out of Hillary.

Thursday, December 24, 2015 at 11:18pm EST

Interesting comments from Jerry Lewis who has a unique take on Trump. *"I think he's great,"* said Lewis.

"He's a showman and we've never had a showman in the president's chair."

Wednesday, December 30, 2015 at 7:33am EST

What is amazing about the Trump campaign is that the man who initially promoted himself as not a politician but a businessman is now acknowledged by the pundits as a great politician. Even Jeb Bush has acknowledged his political skills.

Sunday, January 10, 2016 at 5:59pm EST

If the Trumpster is elected President, will he not use a teleprompter? Wouldn't that be refreshing if he didn't?

Friday, January 15, 2016 at 11:58am EST

Trump and Cruz had a standoff last night. Trump got the best of Cruz on the N.Y. issue. But Cruz trumped the Trump on the birther issue. No matter on the latter because when Trump is trumped all he has to do is give one of his endearingly goofy looks and shrugs and his supporters are happy and the point is forgotten.

Tuesday, January 19, 2016 at 10:59pm EST

"This is going to be so much fun," says Sarah Palin in her endorsement of Trump. This is Trump's appeal; his campaign is fun to watch. He makes everything amusing. The people like it and they like him. Sarah will add even more excitement to the quest for the Presidency.

Sunday, January 24, 2016 at 9:47am EST

Trump does seem consistent in not being concerned about whom he offends. What's with the cussing and multiple use of the F-word in the Vegas rally and speech? Will that offend the evangelicals with whom he and Cruz hope to dance to the nomination? Will the evangelicals give him a slap in the face over his crudeness and take the hand of Cruz? Evangelicals have historically been very strong against use of profanity.

Sunday, January 24, 2016 at 7:53pm EST

Interesting...the Trumpet at church. It would be helpful to have a president who would regularly attend church, especially if he would draw some media people to the service. They need it.

Tuesday, January 26, 2016 at 10:50pm EST

Trump is definitely winning the endorsement battle. Sheriff Joe Arpaio is huge. Now the only thing that could Trump the Trumpster would be if Mr. Conservative, Rush, would endorse Cruz. I doubt if Rush will do it. That is not his way; however, I suspect he may be being pressured from his conservative friends to do so.

Tuesday, January 26, 2016 at 8:22pm EST

I can't help but wonder if Mr. Trump made a very large contribution to Liberty University.

Tuesday, January 26, 2016 at 8:54pm EST

I don't believe it; he will participate. This is another attempt of Trump to dominate the press coverage before the debate. He is skillful in controlling the press coverage, although I think he is in danger of going too far in his attempts to gain and keep the attention focused on the Trumpster. *(Trump did not participate in the debate.)*

Monday, February 8, 2016 at 7:22am EST

In a Trump administration, could Phyllis Schlafly be Secretary of State? She has loyally served the anti-establishment wing of the party. Even though she is 90, she still travels and speaks widely.

Wednesday, February 10, 2016 at 3:01pm EST

The Trumpeter's political incorrectness is appealing; his social correctness leaves something to be desired. Hopefully, if elected, he will moderate his use of profanities and vulgarities. I suppose it makes little difference to most people today. Polite society died years ago. In my experience politicians have a tendency to cuss in private conversation more so than other white collar types. Does it go with power, or what? Trump seems to be the first politician to engage in bad or questionable language in public settings.

Wednesday, February 10, 2016 at 6:21pm EST

I guess I have become the Donald Trump of evangelism.

Thursday, February 11, 2016 at 10:27pm EST

The Trumpster is by far the best dressed of the candidates. I don't like the candidates wearing blue jeans. Trump also has the most presidential demeanor. I like the Trump scowl. Yet, he can have fun at his rallies. I have two Donald Trump dress shirts, which my daughter bought me for my birthday a few years ago.

Build That Wall

Sunday, February 14, 2016 at 10:07am EST
Evidently, I have left the impression with some that I have endorsed Trump. I am not committed as yet to any of the candidates. I have been flirting with Trump. He is the most interesting and exciting one in the field. I do not have to make a decision until the May 6 Indiana primary. I am still playing the field. I could easily support any of the candidates for president over Grandpa 'Burn'ie or Grandma 'Hell'ary. The Governor of Ohio would be my least favorite of the Republicans. He has been around the block too many times and has been seduced by the liberals. Cruz might be the best one to bring home to Mom and Dad.

Monday February 15, 2016
New Mexico State University
About 4 PM a Mexican, who was initially all about love, attacked Joshua, my intern. Joshua responded, "He is why we need to build that beautiful wall." Students warned the assailant that since we were videoing, he could go to jail. The Mexican said, "I have already been to jail." He is the type of Mexican that Trump is trying to keep out of America. Next a black thug, who was also violently against the wall, attacked Joshua. Several students held them back.

The police showed up, one officer said, "It's all over." He ordered Joshua to stop, but he kept preaching. I defended free speech to the police. Meanwhile, Bruce, from the Campus Activities Office, also advocated for our right to speak. The police backed off from stopping us but commanded the students to disperse. Many did leave but we continued speaking to until 5 PM to a group of 10 to 20.

Thursday, February 18, 2016 at 10:00pm EST

"But it came to pass, that when Sanballat [The Pope] heard that we built the wall [refortify Jerusalem], he was wroth, and took great indignation, and mocked the Jews,"--Nehemiah 4:1. There is nothing unchristian about building a wall to protect a nation's borders. Mr. Trump, build that wall!

Monday, February 22, 2016 at 5:06am EST

Why does Trump seem to get more of the evangelical and traditional conservative support than Cruz or Rubio? Even under the presidency of Mr. Conservative himself, Ronald Reagan, the country continued in its mad dash of liberalism and progressiveness. Perhaps the engine was slowed somewhat from what would have been under a Carter or Mondale presidency. However, the engine was not stopped and it certainly was not turned back. The federal government has continued to grow larger and larger under each Republican administration. Despite all the rhetoric, Republican politicians have done virtually nothing to stop abortion, which has been the main issue with evangelicals. Defunding Planned Parenthood would be huge and an action well within legislative powers. But it has not been done.

Cruz is running on a good platform to restore Constitutional government. But he is not resonating like Trump. Regrettably, Americans are no longer schooled enough in the Constitution to see its significance as a campaign issue. Trump's simple undefined slogan, "Make America Great Again" is vibrating.

Of course, if we are going to achieve lasting greatness, a return to the concept of small and limited civil government and individual responsibility is necessary. Big government results in little and weak people. Big people means little government. We need a rugged individualism if we are going to make America great again, an individualism which is rooted in faith in God.

Wait, "rugged individualism" was Hebert Hoover's slogan! That's all right; things have been going downhill since FDR, when internationalism wounded the American Spirit. Limiting the Moslem invasion is Trump's biggest appeal to discontented evangelicals and conservatives. I fear many have given up hoping that anything will be done to stop abortion regardless of who is elected President.

Perhaps stopping the mad followers of Mohammad is the best we can hope for until there is another Great Awakening in America, which I am laboring to bring. A great America must be a Christian America.

Saturday, February 27, 2016 at 11:40pm EST
Donald Trump reminds me of Andrew Jackson, our seventh president, 1829-1837. Trump, like Jackson, is a Presbyterian. Jackson was of Scot/Irish ancestry, Trump is Scot/German. Jackson was known for a volcanic temperament; he killed a man in a duel. And he challenged others to duels and was a noted brawler. If it was legal today, Trump might be a duelist instead of threatening law suits. Jackson's beloved wife, Rachel, was accused of being a bigamist; Trump's wife has been photographed in the nude. Jackson had an unruly shock

of red hair, which was completely gray by the time he became president. Then there is Trump's wild orange hair. Jackson was known as a supporter of the common man. Trump appeals to the blue color class with his populist platform. Jackson was the founder of the Democratic Party; Trump is taking the Republican Party in a new direction. Jackson's political opponents referred to him as a "jackass," which eventually became the symbol of the Democratic Party. Jackson's adversaries also called him a demagogue, referring to him as "King Andrew." Jackson championed transferring power from the political elites to the ordinary voters.

Jackson, like Trump, was a strong nationalist, opposing the threatened secession of South Carolina. Trump is determined to build his great wall. Trump talks tough in defeating ISIS. Jackson was tough in defeating the British at the Battle of New Orleans and the Indians in the Seminole War. Jackson signed the Indian Removal Act; which result in their forced removal to Oklahoma. Trump has promised to remove illegal immigrants. Jackson was one of the most controversial Americans of the 19th Century. "Old Hickory" helped make America great; Trump wants to Make America Great Again.

Monday, March 7, 2016 at 9:02pm EST
If Trump can win with all the opposition from the power elites, it seems like they should not be in the picture in a Trump administration. The question is who would be in the picture besides Donald?

Thursday, March 24, 2016 at 5:58pm EDT
Trump has rewritten the rules of politics.

Thursday, March 24, 2016 at 7:04pm EDT

Trump breaks the rules of politics. Traditionally candidates hide behind staffers, PACS, etc. for their dirty tricks wanting to leave the impression they are above the filth. Trump is upfront; he hides behind no one. Like a pig, he enjoys wallowing in the mud. Just wait until he gets down and dirty with Hillary; even Bill will be no match for the Donald.

Monday, March 28, 2016 at 7:16pm EDT

Former Texas Governor Rick Perry admitted that Donald Trump has "good instincts." Is that what Mr. Trump calls "common sense conservatism?" A caller on Rush today suggested hopefully, "Trump is a conservative in liberal dress." Instead of what he is generally considered by his conservative critics, "A liberal in conservative dress." What sayest my FB friends?

Tuesday, March 29, 2016 at 11:48am EDT

As for the wives becoming an issue in the campaign, why not?

These are days in which women are asserting themselves. We have a woman running for the presidency, who was assertive under her husband's regime.

Mrs. Trump's nude photos had already been published years ago. It may be a little sleazy for Cruz supporters republishing the pictures. So what if Trump responds by comparing his trophy wife with Cruz's more matronly looking wife with an angry countenance? We have seen countless pictures of an angry Hillary.

This will not be the first campaign in which wives have been maligned. Andrew Jackson's political opponents did a number on his wife. After all, this is politics, not church life. It does seem significant that if Trump is elected president his wife will be the first First Lady everyone has had the opportunity to see naked.

Where have you gone Dolly Madison?

Wednesday, March 30, 2016 at 11:52pm EDT
The best word I can think of that describes Mr. Donald J. Trump is that he is an anomaly.

THE DONALD AND BROTHER JED
Thursday March 31, 2016
Texas Tech University

At the end of the day a student told me, "What you do is genius."

Repeatedly, I compared our campus preaching tactics to Donald Trump's approach to campaigning. Our Christian critics listened. Trump says something controversial and CNN is following him all the next day. Trump is high energy and so are we. Christians on campus are more like Jeb Bush, low energy. Trump's rallies are exciting and spontaneous with protesters. Christian student gatherings and Bible studies on campus are typically boring and have virtually no debate, dialogue or disagreement. Trump says something and his opponents all have to spend the next few days responding. The man sets the agenda, not the media, nor the other candidates.

Trump makes politics fun, exciting and memorable. We do the same with religion. Trump is sometimes crude and rude and so are we. After all, we are ministering among vulgar and bad mannered youth.

Trump has all the attention and his opponents resent it. We have the ear of the students more than the professors and campus evangelicals. Trump has brought a lot of new voters into the primary and increased interest in the debates.

Several Christians admitted to me that they had so many more opportunities to witness when we are on campus. One boy, who on Tuesday confronted me about my doctrine of Christian perfection, admitted today that he had had 60 conversations about Christ this week as a result of our preaching. He said to me late in the day, "We are not as far apart in what we believe as I thought."

Friday, April 1, 2016 at 12:47am EDT

Trump is polling terribly among women. I don't put a lot of stock in such polls. I suspect a lot of women secretly like Trump but they will not admit it publically nor even to a pollster. In my experience many women are attracted to the bad boy over the good boy. In actual votes Romney did badly among women. He was too much of a goody two shoes for your typical woman. What naughty woman is going to have any fantasies concerning Romney? In the general election the women will not have a choice of another man. Women don't seem very interested in Hillary, except for some of the old bags from the feminist movement.

It has never been demonstrated in the voting booth that most women actually want a female president. Remember eight years ago women choose a male, Obama, over the one who is supposed to be the feminist darling, Hillary. Romney or someone like Paul Ryan would lose to Hillary because they are gentlemen and they would treat her like a lady. Yet there is little lady-like about the shrew. Trump knows how to tame a shrew.

Finally, men will choose Trump over Hillary. Men might choose a woman over a man if she was a babe, like Palin (eight years ago). But do the Democrats even have any babes to run? Yikes, they have those two witch-like Senators from California and Nancy Pelosi. They would chase away any man. Hillary is over the hill and has been around the block too many times. On the other hand, Trump, despite being 70 years old, is full of energy and is a man's man.

Saturday, April 2, 2016 at 2:52pm EDT

Trump says, "If you are not going to vote for me, don't vote."

Sunday, April 3, 2016 at 6:54pm EDT

Populist is the political term that the media favors to apply to Trump. However, I don't recall Trump himself using or accepting the label. I see Trump as a pragmatist. It is accurate to refer to him as a nationalist as opposed to an internationalist, which has been historically connected with communism. Globalist is the favored term today, which was likely coined to disassociate internationalism from its communist associations.

Trump sees himself as a "deal maker," not an ideologue, which may account for his shifting positions. He may think, why let your opponents know your actual position or for what you will settle before making the deal? Keep others guessing concerning your bottom line.

Wednesday, April 6, 2016 at 8:05pm EDT
If there is a contested convention, we will see how skilled of deal maker Donald Trump actually is.

Thursday, April 7, 2016 at 11:33am EDT
Mr. Trump has called attention to the fact that US taxpayers pay 73% of the costs of NATO. Member nations all need to pay their fair share. Do we even need NATO any longer? Certainly it is not preventing the Muslim invasion of Europe, which is as great a threat if not greater than communism. Europe is mostly socialist anyway.

Mr. Trump should also note the fact that Americans pay almost 1/5 of the costs of the United Nations. It used to be the conservative position that the U.S. should not even be a part of the UN. Mr. Cruz, where are you on the issue of NATO and the UN? "America First" sounds the Trumpet.

Trump vs. Cruz

Monday, April 11, 2016 at 12:40pm EDT
Has Trump been reading from Napoleon's handbook on success in politics? Bonaparte said, "In politics... never retreat, never retract... never admit a mistake."

Monday, April 18, 2016 at 8:22pm EDT
A number of preachers have compared open-air preaching with Trump's campaign style. This is part of the reason I identify with Trump despite things in his past, which I don't like. Trump knows how to handle these human vermin. We are fighting some of the same battles.

Trump has even expressed more tolerance for homosexuals than I; however, these radicals and low-lifes are never satisfied. The more you give into their protests; the more they demand. Trump seems to understand this and he does not take any guff, nor does he have any fear. I like that.

BTW, I like Cruz also. He just does not know how to get the attention that Trump does. Cruz seems to concentrate on operating behind the scenes, which is very important in a campaign and while holding high office.

Tuesday, April 19, 2016 at 5:56am EDT

Trump or Ted? That is the question.

Wednesday, April 20, 2016 at 8:39am EDT

Should Donald Trump become president, he would be the oldest elected to the office for the first time. As far as I have heard his age (70) has not been an issue, since he appears to be so vigorous and energetic. Trump is of my generation, which makes him more appealing to me than Cruz, who is only 45.

Clinton was the first president of my lifetime, who was younger than I. Since him, they have all been youngsters. I am not suggesting age as the most important factor but to me it is a consideration. Age should give men a better perspective on life and issues. We are talking about 25 years of difference between Trump and Cruz, which is quite significant. I also appreciate that Trump does not smoke, drink or take drugs. He doesn't appear to be the type that would take or need mental meds.

Thursday, April 21, 2016 at 8:41pm EDT

OK, the Trumpet sounded an extremely soft note on the bathroom issue thus going PC on us. He released a lot of gas stinking up the place. Cruz took advantage and blew a loud note. Trump may lose us Hoosiers on this one, which could result in a second or third ballot at the convention.

Suddenly, our white knight comes riding into Cleveland. Who shall it be? Curt Shilling is our man, the pitcher with the bloody sock. He lost his job over this issue at ESPN. He needs a position. Kurt Shilling for president.

The Donald redeemed himself a little by supporting Old Hickory on the $20 bill. BTW, where are all the Democrats on defending their first man, Andy Jackson?

Friday, April 22, 2016 at 8:25am EDT

It seems like Hannity thinks he can better explain Trump's position than the candidate. Hannity puts words in Trump's mouth when he doesn't sound as conservative as Hannity thinks he should.

Monday, April 25, 2016 at 5:40pm EDT

Coach Bobby Knight's endorsement of Trump is huge in Indiana. Trump reminds me of the former IU basketball coach in temperament. Knight intimidated referees by throwing chairs and occasionally slapped his players. Both can be foul-mouthed profane men; both are talented and have an imposing presence. Knight was a winner; IU basketball has never been the same after the Knight Era. Both have their avid fans, yet are hated by others. These are men about whom everyone has an opinion.

Tuesday, April 26, 2016 at 10:33pm EDT

Trump is handling questions from the press brilliantly with humor. He connects.

Wednesday April 27, 2016, IUPUI

I decided to go to Indianapolis and preach at IUPUI and afterwards attend the Donald Trump rally at the State Fair Grounds.

Thursday, April 28, 2016 at 5:58am EDT

At his rally in Indianapolis, Mr. Trump introduced Coach Knight, who had contacted Trump months before he decided to be a candidate and urged him to run. Coach Knight informed Trump that he was prepared to help him in anyway. Knight gave him his phone number. In my memory, I cannot remember endorsements having the influence they have had in these primaries. Around Indiana, Bobby Knight is a bigger draw than the CEO from California, Carly Fiorina, Cruz's running mate.

The Coach said, "Donald Trump is the most prepared man in history to be president. There will never be another Benghazi under President Trump."

Knight spoke considerably of Trump's support for the military and for veterans. He stated, "They say he is not presidential. What the hell does that mean? They said the same thing about Harry Truman; yet he was one of the three best presidents we ever had."

Bobby Knight, like Trump, used to frequently slam the media. I remember once when he was asked if he was wearing his "game face," Knight responded, "What the Hell does that mean?" And the Coach began to make many different faces mocking the question. Bobby Knight wore his signature red sweater.

Thursday, April 28, 2016 at 7:30am EDT

No wonder the Republicans always lose the cultural wars even though their constituents often send men to Congress with the right views. Dennis Hastert served as GOP Speaker of the House for eight years. Outwardly, he seemed to be a congenial straight shooter as a former coach. All along he was a pervert. Sinful men have no moral authority.

Thursday, April 28, 2016 at 9:23am EDT

I have to turn in my absentee ballot tomorrow. I have never before been indecisive concerning for whom I will cast my vote. However, I have gone back and forth on the Cruz/Trump option. Ultimately, my decision will be mainly based on which candidate has the most likelihood of defeating Hillary.

I have attended both Cruz and Trump rallies. Trump had thousands more attending his meeting than did Cruz. Of course, Trump's was in a much larger venue, Indianapolis vs. Terre Haute. Trump supporters had much more enthusiasm than Cruz. Cruz did have more substance in his speech. The Carly choice for Cruz's VP adds nothing to attract me to Cruz. Trump has received far more votes than Cruz and the multitudes flock to the Trump rallies, not so with Cruz.

I am not vehemently opposed to either candidate. I have good friends on both sides. On my part I would not reject a friend based on politics.

(I voted Trump in the Indiana primary.)

Thursday, April 28, 2016 at 9:41pm EDT

Patrick J. Buchanan was the forerunner to Donald J. Trump. He prepared the way for Trump when he ran in the New Hampshire primary against Bush in 1992.

Saturday, April 30, 2016 at 4:24pm EDT

I must confess that I understand Trump on this one: Trump doesn't change diapers... "No, I don't do that," Trump said on the Opie and Anthony show in 2005. *"There are a lot of women out there that demand that the husband act like the wife and you know there are a lot of husbands that listen to that...I'm really like a great father but certain things you do and certain things you don't. It's just not for me."*

My mother said to Cindy after we brought five babies into the world, "Jed is the last of a dying breed."

I can relate to the Donald on issues like this. Of course, things change if the husband expects the wife to work outside the home and bring in at least half if not more of the income. Like my father before me, I am old school. Believe it or not, Cindy once told me she actually liked changing diapers. I think I did change a few number 1 diapers. One day, I thought I was going to have to change a number 2 since I could not stand the smell any longer. Thankfully, as I was about to do so, Cindy walked in from grocery shopping. And I went outside for some fresh air and did my usual chore of bringing in the groceries, since I have the muscles.

It should be noted that I bought the labor-saving throw away diapers to lighten Cindy's load. So I always have tried to be a thoughtful husband.

Sunday, May 1, 2016 at 7:04am EDT

Ted Cruz's Constitutionally based message has the substance which America needs. He is to be commended for running a well-organized and articulate campaign. However, slogans like "Make America Great Again" and "I will build that wall" and, "Who is going pay for it?" are winning the day. Trump's campaign has more energy, charisma, theatrics, excitement and emotion, which are the stuff of successful politics. Trump had the advantage from the beginning with his celebrity status. He makes for better press than Cruz. Who knows what Trump will do or say next?

Cruz's message is just not resonating with enough voters among Republicans. Nor would it likely do better in the general election, where a candidate must appeal to Democrats and Independents.

Very few Americans have even read the Constitution. When I was in high school, its study was required by law. I suppose that most Congressmen have not read our founding document that they have sworn to uphold. I wonder if Obama has even read it. Constitutional Law courses emphasize case law, maybe not even reading the document itself. I am assuming Trump probably was required to read it in the prestigious private schools he attended as a boy. Of course, that doesn't necessarily mean he actually read or studied it.

Monday, May 2, 2016 at 5:21am EDT

Yesterday after church, Sister Pat, Joshua and I walked a few blocks to the historical Indiana Theater for a Trump rally in Terre Haute, IN. Already, a multitude was standing in line extending for three blocks. We were among the hundred that were turned away 30 minutes before starting time. Media reported that 2100 people with most standing heard the candidate speak for over an hour.

Last week I went to a Cruz rally in Terre Haute in a venue which seats 1000; no one was turned away, no one was standing and there was considerably less enthusiasm. The contrast says a lot more to me as to who will win Indiana than the polls.

Terre Haute is a Democrat town. Eugene V. Debs, who ran three times for president as a socialist in the early 20th Century, was from Terre Haute.

As I walked the blocks to the end of the line waiting for Trump, the only person I recognized was my mechanic, who owns his own shop. He looked to be the typical class of person attending the rally—the forgotten Americans. I saw no minority types at either the Trump or Cruz rally. Despite Terre Haute being the home of Indiana State University, I observed few who appeared to be academic types or students. There were more families with children at the Trump meeting. There was one protester outside the Trump gathering holding a sign saying something about Nazis.

Thursday, May 5, 2016 at 11:56pm EDT

Donald J. Trump is smart but he is not an intellectual. Ike defeated Adlai Stevenson twice for the presidency. Nixon referred to Stevenson as an egghead. Pseudo intellectuals are not smart, nor do they like Trump. There are true intellectuals like the late William F. Buckley. George Will, who opposes Trump, is a pseudo-intellectual being as he is an atheist. I acknowledge that there are true intellectuals who oppose Trump, like

Thomas Sowell. *(Sowell eventually joined the Trump train.)*

Thursday, May 5, 2016 at 10:58pm EDT

Does Trump's presumptive nomination demonstrate that the party elites, the establishment or the kingpins are not as powerful and influential as some have thought or is his accomplishment a testimony to his political instincts, skills and dominate personality?

VOTING YOUR CONSCIENCE?
Thursday, May 5, 2016

I am tired of hearing that we must follow our consciences in casting or not casting our votes. To vote or not to vote for a particular person is not essentially a moral decision. It is a plan of action, a strategic maneuver, which is usually based more on pragmatism than conscience or principle. Actually, the pragmatic choice can be regarded as a principled choice. Whatever your political persuasion, you are not going to find a pure candidate. It would be rare in casting a vote that there is not some compromise of principle involved. The purist's political influence will be neutralized to the point that he can't vote for anyone who does not completely live up to the standards of Jesus Christ. There has always been an element in the church which refuses to vote at all because they regard politics in general as corrupt.

Some act under the principle of party loyalty, when casting their vote. Loyalty is a noble principle. I have voted for some relatively bad or merely relatively good candidates in my life simply because they are Republicans. I would not vote for a Democrat. Often I have not been that happy with the choices I am offered, but I have never had a guilty conscience, even in voting for a Mormon or for Republican candidates of questionable moral character. Nor have I considered leaving the party since my Republican roots go back generations. I fear my grandfathers, both of whom were Republican politicians, would turn over in their graves if I voted for a Democrat.

Sunday, May 8, 2016 at 2:06pm EDT
It has to be called, "The Great Wall of Trump."

Sunday, May 8, 2016 at 11:59pm EDT
There has been some speculation that Hillary might chose Elizabeth Warren as VP. Should that ticket win the presidency and bring the control of the House back to the Democrats, we would have Hillary, Warren and Nancy Pelosi in charge. That would be a nightmare. Would the Never Trump people still prefer Hillary, even with the phony Indian squaw as the VP candidate? Think about who Witch Hillary would then appoint to the Court--scary. Also there would be the make-up of her cabinet to consider, maybe Boxer or that other female Senator from California. It would be Hell on earth.

Tuesday, May 10, 2016 at 5:27pm EDT
AMAZING PROPHECY ABOUT TRUMP (2011) Firefighter shares vision of President Trump God gave him in 2011. Judgement is not against Citizens but against Leaders of America! *The Spirit of God says, "The enemy will quake and shake and fear this man I have anointed. They will even quake and shake when he announces he is running for president, it will be like the*

*shot heard across the world. The enemy will say what
shall we do now?"*

Wednesday, May 11, 2016 at 12:15pm EDT

It should be kept in mind for the general election that
this is not simply a choice between Trump and Hillary.
The victor will bring a plethora of people to Washington
to serve in the administration. Should Hillary be elected
many of the same ugly faces that ruled in her husband's
administration and others who came with Obama,
including Muslims, will accompany the Mrs. to
Washington. Her administration will include lots of
sodomites. She will likely feel obligated to have some
trans perverts as well. There will be an overload of
bitchy women, who will want to rule over us men,
essentially trying to emasculate any remaining real men
in America.

On the other hand, even if Trump does go more liberal
in the general election as some fear, after winning, he
will have to bring in some of the conservatives such as
Jeff Sessions, who endorsed him early. Also, he has
repeatedly said that evangelicals love him; certainly in
even the worst scenario he will at least throw some sop to
the Christians.

Hopefully, a few conservative women in the tradition
of Phyllis Schlafly will join the Trump administration.
That is if he can find any ladies like Phyllis left. I fear
they are gone with the wind. We may have to settle for
the more foxy blonds, like his daughter. Trump knows
the smartest people. Just ask him, he will tell you. I
suppose most of his appointees will not represent the
political class but business and military leaders. Not

many highbrow academics will be included. It will be interesting to see some fresh faces.

For those who are concerned about such things, a Hillary administration will be no doubt more colorful. But hey, Trump will have Ben Carson. I don't expect Sharpton will have access. That alone is worth sounding the Trumpet. If you don't like Trump, I think you may respect some who will join him in Washington. I don't expect anyone with any sort of conservative orientation would identify with anyone in a Hillary administration. Wouldn't a Chris Christy as say Attorney General be quite an improvement over the two we have had under Obama?

Friday, May 13, 2016 at 11:29am EDT

The Obama administration has issued an order requiring all public schools in the U.S. to allow transgender students access to single-sex bathrooms consistent with their gender identity. What will it take for Americans to take to the streets to stop Obama from continuing to radically change America in the consideration of this latest attempt to break down our culture and morals? Parents, it is time to take your children out of the government schools in protest. Enough is enough! If this does not convince parents that the government's mission is to corrupt and rape their children, what will?

Either put your children in a private school or else home school. If parents would do so, we can stop this. Alas, too many mothers are pursuing their careers and fathers are failing to support their families to make a meaningful protest. Some of us have been sounding the alarm for years. Wake up! Who Will Rise Up? State and local officials, it is time to make a statement and refuse federal funds, even though it is our own money that Obama threatens to withdraw from the schools. Spirit of '76, where have you gone?

Trumping the Race Card

Friday, May 13, 2016 at 9:46am EDT

Good interview with fellow Hoosier, Dan Quayle, whom I have always respected. Unfortunately, the media did a number on him. Brother Quayle wisely answers the questions in this interview concerning Trump. Quayle would have made a good president.

Friday, May 27, 2016 at 6:49am EDT

Interesting article, an example of what Trump says, "We don't win anymore." Of course, one must fight to win.

THE MORTAL WOUNDING OF THE P.C. MOVEMENT
Tuesday, May 31, 2016,
University of California Davis

I pressed the politically correct buttons of the females, including the racial buttons. I announced that the PC movement has been mortally wounded with the ascent of Donald J. Trump as the leader of the Republican Party and the death blow will be struck when he is elected president, which alone will be a great accomplishment.

We will then even be able to tell ethnic jokes once again. It may also spell the end of the press dominating politics and setting the political agenda.

Saturday, June 4, 2016 at 8:55am EDT

"The Louisville Lip" with his provocative and outrageous talk paved the way for the acceptance of a political celebrity personality like Donald Trump. Cassius Clay knew how to control press conferences and interviews and expound on issues other than boxing. He was not afraid to rattle the white establishment of his day. Prior to Clay, it was not acceptable for athletes or men in general to be such braggers. Clay's reputation as "the greatest" was initially a self-label.

Trump is an outstanding self-promoter, which provides great press coverage, which has enabled him to become the Republican Standard Bearer and may well carry him to the Presidency. Boxer Clay turned into an international ambassador. Businessman Trump may become leader of the free world. If there had been no Clay, there would have been no "The Donald," at least as we know him today. *(Written upon the passing of Mohammed Ali, AKA Cassius Clay.)*

Wednesday, June 8, 2016 at 6:49pm EDT

Mexican is not a race. It is a nationality. Race has to do with genetics. I would not expect to be treated fairly by a Muslim judge, especially if he is true to the teachings of Sharia Law. There is nothing wrong with being Mexican; it is wrong to be a Muslim. However, neither is a racial issue. The reporter may be considered a racist by wanting to turn Trump's criticism of the judge into a racial issue.

Saturday, June 11, 2016 at 12:30pm EDT

Racist is a loaded term. Men like Romney use the term but do not define it. Mexican is a nationality, not a race.

Obama and the Democrats made Obama's race a major factor in two elections. Romney did not accuse Obama of being racist. Romney is an ingrate. He asked all Republicans to rally around him, now he does not want to back the party nominee, even though Trump supported Romney in 2012. Oh well, who needs this loser anyway?

Tuesday, June 14, 2016 at 8:00pm EDT
Trump's got them "all shook up!" Good for him. Plain talk and common sense has been a long time coming. Go, Donald, Go!

Friday, June 17, 2016 at 10:13am EDT
Some GOP leaders are still trying to find a way to stop Trump from becoming the party's nominee. If elected President, would Democrats unite with Republicans by daringly attempting to prevent him from taking the oath of office?

Wednesday, June 22, 2016 at 4:53pm EDT
Could any of Mr. Trump's critics give me an example of anything that he has said or done that is racist?

Saturday, June 25, 2016 at 3:39pm EDT
Does anyone know if any critics of the evangelicals who had the meeting with Mr. Trump were issued an invitation to the meeting? I would be impressed if these critics were invited, then declined.

Friday, June 24, 2016 at 7:45am EDT
I have not studied this issue of Britain leaving the European Union, but my gut reaction is that it is good for England. It is a major blow to globalism and the New

World Order. Therefore, it is good for America and the rest of the world. It is a loss to internationalists like Obama and Hillary. It is a victory for nationalism and it prepares the way for Donald Trump to Make America Great Again! It seems especially positive for all English speaking people.

Saturday, June 25, 2016 at 2:58pm EDT

Does anyone know of any Muslims who have Trump's ear?

Monday, June 27, 2016 at 9:56am EDT

I was surprised that Dr. Dobson would make the report of Donald J. Trump's acceptance of Jesus Christ as his Savior public, especially considering it is second hand information and that Trump is so much in the public eye. In my experience someone may repeat "the sinner's prayer" more than once before he comprehends the magnitude of his decision. A sinner may make a private decision before he is prepared to make it public. All of us at times have probably become caught up in our zeal and hope for converts to speak of someone's conversion before we have observed the fruit of repentance or given time for the fruit to manifest. I suspect that Dobson believes that repentance follows the new birth instead of it being a prerequisite for the experience. We should all appreciate the work that Dr. Dobson has done to promote and preserve the family unit.

Thursday, June 30, 2016 at 10:55am EDT

"POLL: Trump pulls into lead 43 to 39," reads the Drudge headline. I am tired of the media treating elections as horse races. Poll numbers at this stage are pretty meaningless. We haven't even had the conventions yet or any face to face debates. What would the media talk about if they did not constantly analyze the polls? Let the candidates speak instead of the boring pundits pushing the polls. The only poll that counts is on Election Day.

The pundits say this candidate or that one has had a bad week. It's all mostly spin either from the candidates or the media, including The Factor. It used to be that the general election campaign did not even really start until after Labor Day.

Thursday, June 30, 2016 at 7:52pm EDT

Trump's critics regularly accuse him of being a narcissist and egotist, usually there are strong adjectives accompanying these accusations. The implication is that Trump has a mental disorder. I see Trump as having great self-confidence and I perceive him as a man of faith. I am not saying he has saving faith but he does demonstrate the faith that has enabled him to move mountains in the business world. And his faith strengthened him to run away from 16 Republicans, who were mostly more prominent than he in the political world.

Trump's faith was inspired by his pastor, Norman Vincent Peale. Dr. Peale had a long running radio program called *"The Art of Living."* I don't think it is a coincidence that Trump entitled his book, *"The Art of the Deal."* Trump's life demonstrates the power of positive thinking. Unfortunately, Trump has not always applied these principles to every area in his life. But I will let his detractors make those points.

Tuesday, July 5, 2016 at 8:38pm EDT

I respect Newt Gingrich for coming out early in support of Trump. Newt is probably the most articulate choice that Trump could make for VP. However, Newt is older than Trump and he has been around too long. I would like to see Trump go outside the box and pick Alan West. If not, as a Hoosier our favorite son, Governor Pence, would work.

Newt certainly should be given a significant position in a Trump administration. President Trump would bring a lot of fresh faces to Washington, not true with Hillary; we pretty much know what we would get. Worst of all would be her husband. Alas, she would be worse than her husband ever was. At least Bill is likeable in a carnal sort of way. Trump likes to surprise; West would be a surprise and remarkable choice.

Thursday, July 7, 2016 at 10:25am EDT

Jesus has given the church great power: *Matt 16:18-19, "And I tell you that you are Peter, and on this rock I will build my church, and the gates of Hades will not prevail against it. I will give you the keys of the kingdom of heaven. Whatever you bind on the earth will be bound in heaven, and whatever you loose on earth will be loosed in heaven."*...Trump is right we need to exercise such power and be the head not the tail.

The Donald and Constantine the Great

Thursday, July 7, 2016 at 2:17pm EDT

Pastor Craig Rogers wrote the following: *I see similarities with the Donald to Constantine. The latter was a great leader who did tremendous good not only for the kingdom of Byzantium but for the whole world. Like Donald, his own relationship with the Living Christ was questionable through most of his life (until near his death when he was baptized), yet he was very favorable towards the Christian faith and protected it. Donald has been very positive towards the Christian faith and has promised to protect it. It seems that the hand of God was with Constantine in his every endeavor. He was quite successful in all that he did. Success is from the Lord.*

The Donald has been successful in his endeavors. Even his business failings were used by him for further success in other businesses.

There were two other "Augusti" (co-regents with Constantine in the Roman Empire just before its transition into Byzantium) who each tried to take over the kingdom. Constantine defeated both. Those other two Augusti were wicked. One was a hater of the Christian faith. If one of those two had been victorious, how different the world would be now. Presently, the other presidential candidate is wicked. We need a Constantine now.

Thursday, July 7, 2016 at 6:32pm EDT

Ted Cruz has agreed to speak at the convention. Donald and Ted embraced today and firmly shook hands. Mrs. Cruz also embraced Mr. Trump. Evidently, there are no hard feelings. I hope those who promoted the virtue of Cruz will follow his example and embrace Trump. He is no longer "Lyin' Ted;" he is "Lovin' Ted." Cruz is doing what loyal party politicians do after a rough primary; they support the candidate of the party.

Sunday, July 10, 2016 at 8:02am EDT

A few days ago I suggested Alan West as a good choice for Trump's VP. Sheriff Clark would be an even better pick. Nixon won in '68 on a strong law and order platform, when there was rioting in the streets. Trump needs to pick someone that the left fears. For if Trump should be elected, the Democrats would soon go for impeachment, if not something worse. They had to get rid of Spiro Agnew before they forced Nixon to resign.

If there is one thing liberals can't stand, it is a black conservative. They don't fear the likes of Newt; he is an establishment figure, who could even turn on Trump. Trump likes winners. West lost his bid for re-election to Congress. Sheriff Clark is a winner, who could help Trump the most with non-whites. And you know how women fall for men in uniform. They would flock to a Trump/Clark ticket. I am not convinced that most women really want a woman president, especially one who is so, well you know, the "b" word.

Thursday, July 14, 2016 at 9:12pm EDT

Instead of a new and unique candidate for president in American history as some say, I would regard Trump as a throwback candidate, who represents the thinking of your typical candidate from either party prior to the mid-20th Century and certainly in 19th Century. As for Trump's treatment of women and minorities, does he oppose women's suffrage? Does he own any slaves? Did Trump ever kill any Indians? Excuse me; I should say "Native Americans." Does he endorse or condone Jim Crow laws? Does he advocate putting Muslims in concentration camps like FDR did with the Japanese in WWII?

Thursday, July 14, 2016 at 4:24pm EDT

Well, I see that Judge Ginsburg has apologized for her remarks concerning Donald Trump. Even the NY Times and Washington Post thought she was out of line. I can't remember the last time a liberal has been pressured to apologize for anything said or done.

Thursday, July 14, 2016 at 10:36am EDT

I would like Trump to surprise us by picking someone who has not been on his long or short list. I would not put it past him.

Monday, July 18, 2016 at 9:04am EDT

The Sheriff Clark put this boy reporter in his place. The Sheriff is mad and he ought to be. The reporter has the audacity to tell the Sheriff to hold the volume down. The Sheriff ends up questioning the reporter, who refuses to condemn all the anti-police venom from the mouths of Black Lives Matter. The Sheriff is speaking tonight at the Republican Convention. What place should he hold in the Trump administration?

Monday, July 18, 2016 at 10:46pm EDT

Now that Mrs. Trump has taken the stage after being in the background up until this time, Hillary is finished. Mr. and Mrs. Trump and Mike Pence cannot lose. Mrs. Trump gave a wonderful speech. Despite the youthful indiscretions of some of her modeling poses, she has a modest demeanor. Watch this woman; she will make a big difference in this campaign. She is Trump's ace that he has been holding back. But now she is in the game. One thing about The Donald, he has timing.

Monday, July 18, 2016 at 8:10pm EDT

I missed the Rabbi who opened the convention in prayer. Willie Robertson started his speech with a prayer in Jesus' name. He says Trump will have our back, if you are a businessman, soldier, cop, or if you are just an average person. He says we can trust Trump to Make America Great Again. Scot Baio is speaking now, an actor; I never heard of him.

Monday, July 18, 2016 at 11:42pm EDT

Pastor Paula White presented a strong closing prayer. James Dobson reported that she (White) prayed with Trump some years ago for the salvation of his soul.

Tuesday, July 19, 2016 at 1:16pm EDT

Mrs. Trump's whole demeanor and tone is as different as, well, as the difference between white and black, when compared to Michele Obama. Obviously, Michele has a chip on her shoulder and does not have a love for America as does Mrs. Trump. Michele said in 2008, after Democrats began to rally around her husband, "For the first time in my adult life I am proud of my country." Mrs. Trump was proud enough of America to move here by choice and patriotic enough to become a citizen.

No one will ever accuse Melania of being a "tranny." I mean we have all had the opportunity to see Mrs. Trump almost naked. She is no transsexual that is for sure. The alternative to Mrs. Trump is unthinkable. Bill Clinton as first man posing naked, perish the thought! Let's just hope he can keep his pants on should Hillary by some trickery win the Presidency. Hillary better insist that there will only be male interns in her White House.

Tuesday, July 19, 2016 at 5:29pm EDT

Cindy and I have been listening to the audio version of *"The Art of the Deal."* I believe it gives good insight into Donald Trump's campaign for the Presidency. What Trump did as a businessman, he continues in his role as candidate Trump and will likely proceed as President Trump.

Schwartz, as Trump's ghost writer, is unethical to deny Trump credit for the book. Trump gave Schwartz recognition for his contribution, whatever it may have been. The author line on the cover of the book says, "Donald J. Trump with Tony Schwartz." Trump's name is not larger than Schwartz's. Many authors, who contract with ghost writers, give them no credit.

The book is Trump's life as he sees it or as he wants others to understand it. Tony Schwartz admits he lied about Trump in "The Art of the Deal" for money. Why should we believe him today? Swartz criticizes Trump's use of hyperbole. Yet Schwartz is quoted in the New Yorker article as saying, "I genuinely believe that if Trump wins and gets the nuclear codes, there is an excellent possibility it will lead to the end of civilization." This statement sounds like hyperbole to me. I doubt if Schwartz literally believes that the election of Trump will be that dire. Is Schwartz lying? No, I would not consider this a lie, but an exaggeration to voice his opposition of Trump in a dramatic and memorable way.

Evidently, Trump is not a reader. Back in the 80's, he read the NY Times daily; however, people don't read newspapers anymore, we all get our news though TV or the Internet. Trump is a doer. He is a man of action. As for Trump's short attention span, this comes out in his book and public persona. Trump is focused when he needs to be. He instinctively grasps situations that might take hours for other men to discern. An experienced man can cut to the core of an issue quickly and move on to something else.

Most books by celebrities and politicians are ghost written. More books than we realize are ghost written. Many books by prominent writers are ghost written in order to keep up with consumer demands for the author's works. College professors often have their free ghost writers, graduate students. A good ghost writer takes the thoughts and ideas of his subject and writes them in an organized manner.

Even if Schwartz did virtually all the writing; his words were likely considerably edited by the publisher before the work appeared in print. It is Trump's autobiography; he can present himself in the manner that he wants. There are biographies one can read of Trump and countless articles. If Trump wins the Presidency, this election will likely become the most written about election in American history.

Many of Trump's Republican rivals tried to pass him off as a secret or shadow liberal. I watched the Convention from gavel to gavel last night. Or should I say from prayer to prayer? I did not hear anything that could be construed as liberal. Trump has chosen a social conservative as his VP and I don't know that Trump has significantly backed off in any of his public stands.

The conventional wisdom for a Republican is to be conservative in the primaries and shift to the center in the general election. So far, we have not seen this shift in Trump, nor promotion of liberalism. No doubt in the past Trump has taken some liberal stances on issues and voiced his support of liberal politicians. Could it just be as Trump has said, "It was the price of doing business in a place like N.Y.," which is dominated by liberalism? There is little that is conventional about Donald J. Trump.

Tuesday, July 19, 2016 at 5:54pm EDT

What? Some woman just offered a Sikh prayer opening the Convention. She wore a covering and spoke in some tongue than gave the interpretation, I guess. Actually, there was nothing wrong with what she said, but it was not offered up to the true God. Last night a rabbi gave the invocation. I suppose that is why the first speaker, Willie Robertson, opened with a prayer offered to the Father, in Jesus' name.

Tuesday, July 19, 2016 at 6:00pm EDT

Jeff Sessions put Trump's name into nomination. And rightly so, he was one of the first prominent Republicans to get on the Trump train.

Tuesday, July 19, 2016 at 7:02pm EDT

I remember that in years long gone by, when the chairman gave the roll call at the convention, the spokesman delegate of a state would cry, "The great SOVEREIGN State (whatever state) casts its votes for _____ _____ the next President of the United States." The word sovereign always impressed me.

So far I have not heard one delegate use the word "Sovereign." Alas, I fear we have lost the concept. Since the mid-20th Century, the federal government has become so powerful, that the states are no longer sovereign. Hopefully, a Trump presidency will bring us back to the Constitutional principles of the limited and defined powers of the federal government and back to the 9th and 10th Amendments.

Tuesday, July 19, 2016 at 10:27pm EDT

Wow, I sense the beginning of a family dynasty to lead America into the future. Any father would be blessed to have a son who could give such a ringing endorsement of his father's accomplishments, skills and character.

Junior has five children and is evidently the husband of only one wife. What I have observed of the public behavior of Donald Trump's offspring is impressive. The blond daughter (did not catch her name), who just graduated from college demonstrated much poise and admiration of her father in her speech as well.

Wednesday, July 20, 2016 at 3:46pm EDT

The music at the Republican convention does not represent traditional values. How about some patriotic marches of John Philip Sousa?

Wednesday, July 20, 2016 at 7:49pm EDT

Tonight a Mormon gave the invocation. So far we have had a Jew, a Sikh and now a Mormon. At least the Mormon opened by addressing the Heavenly Father and closed his petition in the name of the Son of God, Jesus Christ. He also made reference to the Atonement of Christ. The prayer is followed with some degenerate rock 'n roller screaming. Anybody know who this screamer is?

Wednesday, July 20, 2016 at 11:49pm EDT

I am so glad I voted for Trump over Cruz. Cruz's failure to endorse Trump tonight was a confirmation to me that Trump was the man all along. Plus there are the intangibles like Trump has much more of a stage presence then Cruz, which, like it or not, can make a significant difference in an election. Ultimately, I voted for Trump because I thought he could defeat Hillary and Cruz would probably not. Cruz's appeal was too narrow.

Thursday, July 21, 2016 at 9:35am EDT

Peter Thiel, co-founder of PayPal, is one of the prime time speakers tonight. He heads an organization that gives promising students $100,000 to drop out of college. Good idea! I am afraid that college often destroys the three I's crucial to success, Initiative, Industriousness, and Independence. The university mentality is to get a job instead of promoting entrepreneur skills, which open and provide job opportunities for others. Thiel's support of the Great Entrepreneur demonstrates that it is OK to vote for Trump, even if you are gay.

Thursday, July 21, 2016 at 7:57pm EDT

Jerry Falwell, Jr. -- As President of the renowned Liberty University, his early endorsement was key in capturing the evangelical vote for Trump. *"Trump is one of the greatest visionaries of our times."* Falwell has never met such a beautiful and loving family as the Trumps.

Chapter 2

General Election

"But Christianity is under tremendous siege... But you know the fact is that there is nothing the politicians can do to you if you [Christians] band together. You have too much power. But the Christians don't use their power... We have to strengthen. Because we are getting — if you look, it's death by a million cuts — we are getting less and less and less powerful in terms of a religion, and in terms of a force... if I'm there, you're going to have plenty of power," Donald Trump, Iowa, Jan. 2016.

Thanking the Church

Friday, July 22, 2016 at 7:16pm EDT

Last night Mr. Trump expressed his thankfulness for support from the church and expressed that it was a big reason for him gaining the nomination. Notice his humility in acknowledging that he may not be worthy of their help:

"At this moment, I would like to thank the evangelical and religious community because I'll tell you what, the support they have given me, and I'm not sure I totally deserve, it has been so amazing and has had such a big reason for me being here tonight... They have so much to contribute to our politics, yet our laws prevent you from speaking your minds from your own pulpits. An amendment, pushed by Lyndon Johnson, many years ago, threatens religious institutions with a loss of their tax-exempt status if they openly advocate their political views. Their voice has been taken away. I am going to work very hard to repeal that language and protect free speech for all Americans."

Friday, July 22, 2016 at 8pm EDT

Post from the wife: *God is raising up Donald Trump to say and do what most Christian men including politicians and ministers refuse to do, like fight for free speech even for Christians. He is the first one I have ever heard suggest repealing the laws that prohibit a church from endorsing a candidate! Go Trump! I also like the way he humbly admitted that he did not deserve the evangelical vote.*

As a campus preacher, free speech is important, even though many Christians rarely exercise the right so they might not miss it. Obama so twisted Title 9 that campus police tried to use it to stop us from preaching at LSU and other campuses.

I hate to see what new "guidelines" Hell Dog Hillary would send to the campuses if she is elected. The campuses must follow the regulations or lose federal funds. A vote for Trump is a vote to get the Gospel to the college students of America!!

Monday, July 25, 2016 at 1:30pm EDT

Last week I left my large print Bible at a church in Arkansas. Therefore, I have been reading one of my retired Bibles, which I was using in 2008 during McCain's campaign for president. Should I cover this sticker (on the Bible) with a Trump sticker? Or is either man's name on the cover profaning the Sacred Writ? Establishment Republicans asked conservatives, who had reservations concerning McCain to rally around the party's nominee. And we did. Eight years later some establishment Republicans, like Bush, will not support Trump despite the alternative of Hillary the Terrible, who could possibly be even worse than Obama.

Monday, July 25, 2016 at 2:32pm EDT

Wow, a progressive saying, "Trump is going to flatten you like a pancake, Hillary." My good friend, Rocket, from Columbia, MO, who is an evangelical Catholic with progressive political leanings, tells me he is voting for Trump. Rocket knows the progressive community in Columbia as well as anyone. He recently told me that same thing; 80% of progressives he knows will not vote for Hillary. He mentioned that many will vote for the Green Party candidate.

I like what one man says in this clip, *"The only people who like Hillary is CNN."*

I have rarely met a student who said *she* likes Hillary. I have never heard one that said that *he* likes Hillary.

Monday, July 25, 2016 at 2:49pm EDT

Now Hillary has tweeted, "Vote your Conscience." Jill Stein the Green Party candidate says, "Vote your values." Cruz also said, "Vote your conscience. Plain spoken Trump says, "Vote for me."

Tuesday, July 26, 2016 at 9:21pm EDT

The sentence quoted in the headline leaves a false impression that Mr. Trump is irreligious, which he is not. He essentially says, when he does wrong he just tries to make it right by changing his behavior. Too many Christians confess to God for their wrongdoing but do not change. This is worse than not bringing God into the equation. Trump does bring God into his experience by taking Communion, which is an acknowledgement of Christ's death for our sins.

The Temperament

Tuesday, July 26, 2016 at 10:54pm EDT

Donald Trump reminds me of Ty Cobb, who is arguably the greatest who ever played the game of baseball and the first player to be inducted into the Hall of Fame. Cobb was known for his aggressiveness and unpredictability. He was not only a great hitter [367 lifetime batting average] but always a threat to steal a base.

Cobb said, *"The base paths belonged to me, the runner. The rules gave me the right. I always went into a bag full of speed, feet first. I had sharp spikes on my shoes. If the baseman stood where he had no business to be and got hurt, that was his own fault."*

Cobb said, *"Most of all I was saddling that [the opposing] team with a psychological burden so that they would be muttering, 'Cobb is crazy.' He'll run anytime and in any situation. It would help give them the jitters and they'd concentrate so much on me they were not paying any attention to the business at hand. My failures rarely were complete failures. They were more like future investments."*

Cobb was known as a hard negotiator for his annual salary with the Detroit Tigers. After retirement, he became baseball's first millionaire through wise investments in the stock market.

Cobb was a winner, *"I never could stand losing. Second place didn't interest me. I had a fire in my belly."*

Trump is a winner and he certainly is not going to be defeated by a female.

Wednesday, July 27, 2016 at 3:53pm EDT
Oh boy, Trump really has them shook up today. You gotta love this guy! He is stealing the stage from Hillary. I think the glass ceiling cracked her head long ago.

Sunday, July 31, 2016 at 12:57pm EDT
Jed Smock shared Dave Daubenmire's post.

Dave Daubenmire has become one of the leading spokesman on the Internet against the Never Trump people of the Christian right. He is no cream puff. When we were living in Central Ohio, he was fired from his football coaching job at Lakewood High School in Ohio for praying with his team. He has paid his dues and is a notable Christian activist for many causes. Like Mr. Trump, Coach Dave is plain spoken.

Wednesday, August 3, 2016 at 1:40pm EDT
Trump shouts, "The Emperor has no clothes!" And all hell breaks loose against him.

Thursday, August 4, 2016 at 3:49pm EDT
Trump is the Clint Eastwood of the business/political world. They represent the epitome of manliness to multitudes of Americans. Can you believe that Eastwood actually called Kahn a "poor slob?" Trump and Eastwood can be raw. Some of us remember Eastwood from his youthful days as Rowdy Yates on "Rawhide," which was my favorite TV show when I was a boy.

Friday, August 5, 2016 at 2:44pm EDT
If Trump is insane for "attacking" a gold star family, how much more is Hillary for lying to the families of those killed in Benghazi. She told them it was all about a video when all the time she knew otherwise. Then Hillary had the audacity to call the gold star mother a liar.

Friday, August 5, 2016 at 7:08pm EDT
Please explain how Hillary has a better "temperament" to be president than Trump.

Saturday, August 6, 2016 at 11:55am EDT
Throughout most of our history a woman was thought not to have the temperament to be president or to participate in politics or even to vote. Who does Hillary think she is to question Trump's temperament? He's the man!

Sunday, August 7, 2016 at 12:54am EDT
Once again Trump handles a situation with grace and humor. The media doesn't get it because they have neither. Nothing wrong with the way he handled the Purple Heart gift either.

Sunday, August 7, 2016 at 8:23pm EDT
https://the-politik.com/2016/08/04/trump_will_win_landslide/

Tuesday, August 9, 2016 at 7:03pm EDT
The media's bias against Trump, especially since he received the Republican nomination, has been blatant. However, I am not convinced that it will remain that bad. Jim Rutenberg's article in the NY Times has been widely circulated. He admits to bias reporting against Trump, excusing it because in the minds of most journalists Trump is a grave danger to our Republic. However, in the long run the media is more interested in promoting itself than in the well-being of our Republic.

Does the media really want the Trump phenomenon to end on November 8? Trump provides great press, much more so than Hillary. The ink press is all about selling newspapers and magazines. Television news is about getting the highest ratings. A lot more people will listen to a Trump interview or speech than they will to Hillary.

Hillary puts everyone to sleep. And when she tries to rev it up, she is shrill. I doubt if Hillary will give any more press conferences as president than she does as a candidate. Trump has been the leading story over the last year. Like it or not, a Trump presidency will be much more exciting than a replay of the Clinton administration of the 90's. Hillary will bring the same old retreads of the 90's with her to Washington. The only new faces will be Muslims that no one really likes. Whereas Trump will bring new people, the best people, the smartest people. Most of the old Republican standbys will no longer have favor in a Trump administration. Of course, Trump will have some obligations to the old guard, like Newt and "America's Mayor." The Bushes will finally be buried.

If Trump wins, it will be the most written about election in our history as the man who comes out of nowhere to win the presidency with significant opposition from his own party. It will be the big event of America's electoral history. From a historical point of view, the idea of Hillary being the first woman president so far has not seemed to capture the imagination of the electorate as Obama being the first black president.

Trump is quotable and unpredictable; Hillary is boring and predictable. Old Bill is probably getting too old to have sex scandals, which always captures the attention of the media and the masses. Does Hillary have any sex appeal at all? On the other hand, Trump remains an energetic rock star at 70, comparable to Mick Jagger, who still has his moves, even though he is older than the Trumpster.

Trump has a young and dynamic family. There is no comparison between Ivanka and Chelsea. Would the world prefer stories concerning the first gentleman, Bill Clinton, or the first lady, Melania Trump? Can you imagine Bill giving a tour of the White House, *"Now it was under this desk in the Oval Office that a major news story developed. . ."* We have heard it over and over, Bill; the American people are tired of the Clintons and all the scandals.

Wednesday, August 10, 2016 at 12:45pm EDT

It is really a stretch to see Trump's comments as a veiled assassination threat. If Hysterical Hillary is elected Trump will be out of the picture immediately. On the other hand, when Hillary the Horrible does go after the citizens' weapons, many NRA people will see it as grounds to take up arms. If there is any sort of threat in Trump's humor, defense against despots is what Trump had in mind. The final step in conquering people is to disarm the people, second amenders understand this. Guns are primarily to protect us from tyrants not for sport.

Wednesday, August 10, 2016 at 8:42am EDT

Is there a more conservative Republican president or nominee since Reagan than Trump? If so, who? Trump's latest speech on the economy spoke of lowering taxes, deregulation and building the pipe line. These are basic conservative policies. He is as strong an advocate of building up the military as anybody since Reagan.

Wednesday, August 10, 2016 at 9:52pm EDT

The Donald has the liberal media and a good number of Republicans in a frenzy again. I love it! Do these people really believe he was encouraging second amenders to assassinate Hilary or are they just putting on a self-righteous act hoping to "kill and bury" (oops, I mean discredit) Trump? I like Trump's sense of humor. Trump is the man.

Thursday, August 11, 2016 at 4:55pm EDT

The Trumpster is doubling down on Hillary and the media, calling Obama and Hillary founder and co-founder of ISIS. Our guy is determined to stay on the attack. No politician in my memory has taken on the media like Trump since Spiro Agnew. I've got Trump's back. How about you, FB friend?

Thursday, August 11, 2016 at 10:21pm EDT

When David brought the Ark of the Lord back to Jerusalem, he took off his royal robes and shouted, leaped, danced and played with the common people. His wife, Michal, mocked him for being undignified and shameful in the eyes of the handmaidens of his servants.

David said unto Michal, *"It was before the Lord, who appointed me to be a ruler over his people. Therefore will I play before the Lord. And I will yet be more vile than this, and will be base in mine own sight: and of the maidservants which thou hast spoken of shall I be had in honor."* Therefore, God punished Michal by making her childless unto her death, --2 Samuel 6:21-23.

Expect Trump to get even "more vile" as Election Day approaches. He is fighting the Philistine [Democrat] enemy, Obama, Hillary, Wolf Blitzer and his media gang.

Michal should have been loyal and rejoiced with David that the Ark was back in Jerusalem. Trump's fellow Republicans are disloyal to the Party and are constantly mocking him for his vulgarity and undignified comments and ways.

When Trump is honored by the people with the presidency, his Republican detractors will pay the price, including some of the old guard on Fox News. If he loses, he will have had the time of his life shouting what Republicans have been fearful of proclaiming for half a century or more.

Friday, August 12, 2016 at 6:31pm EDT

"I was being sarcastic, but not all that sarcastic to be honest with you," classic Donald Trump.

Friday, August 12, 2016 at 8:14pm EDT

Trump reminds me of a famous 19th Century American, who was a politician, newspaper publisher, businessman, showman and entertainer. He was well known internationally. He started as a Democrat then switched to the Republican Party. He gained prominence and success when he was living in N.Y. City. Also, he was a teetotaler. He was very wealthy and owned several mansions. Anyone know of whom I am writing?

Shawn Harding: *Abraham Lincoln?*

Jessica Romero: *Hearst?*

Rick Farwell: *Horace Greeley?*

Timothy Duane Davis: *Samuel Langhorne Clemens, "Mark Twain,"*

Rick Farwell: *That was going to be my next guess.*

Cheryl Clayton: *Do tell!*
Jed Smock: *Think showman and promoter.*
Kaley Graves: *P.T. Barnum. The circus guy.*
Rick Farwell: *That's gotta be it!*
Jed Smock: *Yes, P.T. Barnum*
Kaley Graves: *He's a cool guy. I studied him in high school once.*

Sunday, August 14, 2016 at 5:46pm EDT

Maybe it's time for the Trump campaign to boycott CNN. Not allow them in his rallies and for campaign spokesmen to not grant interviews to the Clinton News Network. After all Hillary has essentially blocked network coverage by not even having press conferences. Her rallies are as boring as Hades.

DONALD TRUMP,
A MAN AFTER MY OWN HEART
Tuesday August 16, 2016

Donald Trump is daily accused by Democrats and Republicans alike of being undisciplined and off message. "He needs to stick to the script," they say. They do not understand his satire and irony. If they do understand, they do not appreciate his unique approach to political campaigning. The fact is, the Donald is very disciplined and focused on his message. The real problem is that his critics hate his core message, "Make America Great Again!"

During the primaries he was outspent by many of his more politically prominent opponents, yet he easily defeated them all. Still, the pundits don't get it.

As an open-air campus preacher, I understand Donald Trump. Much of the criticism of my ministry comes from the Christian community, who should be supportive. They say, *"Just preach the gospel. We have been listening all day and have not heard the name of Jesus once. Stick to the Bible. Don't talk about politics, economics, philosophy, psychology, etc."*

The fact is that I do regularly refer to the death and resurrection of Jesus. I repeatedly declare that Jesus is the only way to salvation. The problem is students have ears, but they hear not. They cannot handle it when we smash their intellectual idols and convict their consciences with the power of the Holy Ghost.

Virtually daily Trump makes seemingly outrageous statements. We preachers are daily accused of being offensive. We mock unbelievers' so called lifestyles and worldly values. To an extent we are showmen. We do not have a captive audience like the professors, but at least we do have the ear of the students. With our confrontational style of evangelism, we force the Christian community further and further into the background of irrelevance. They are losing their small corner. They accuse me, "You are ruining everything we have been working for all year." Their work is peaceful coexistence with humanism and secularism.

Trump dominates the media. Meanwhile, Hillary stays in the background afraid to duel it out with Trump, which is wise on her part since she does not come near having his charisma. And her message is without substance. It is the same old, same old, from the Obama years and the same socialist's stuff going back to her husband's administration with all the scandals. Trump has a new and refreshing message that captures the attention of the populace. "I will build the wall and make Mexico pay for it!"

Trump has to go it alone or so it seems. I have been going it alone for over four decades. Neither one of us are actually alone. Both of us have our supporters but they are unseen. There is a definite method to our apparent madness. But men refuse to see it. They do not want to believe what we say. Trump is a threat to the established order of both political parties. We are a threat to the university because if what we say is true, then most of what is being taught at the university is false.

Sister Cindy and I understand that the gospel includes freedom from sin. Christians on campus share a gospel that forgives sin but does not set free from the power and dominion of sin. They hate this aspect of Christ's message, which is the core of his message. When Trump speaks, both the politicians and media are worked into a frenzy. He says what no one else dares to say. What he says seems outrageous but in reality it is not. It is so offensive because the abnormal has become the normal in our society and especially on college campuses. Neither Trump nor I accept the politically correct thinking of this generation, whether it is in the general society or the church.

When I preach, the sinners and professing Christians are emotionally agitated and rarely engage us intellectually. Likewise, neither the media nor Hillary will rationally engage the man so loudly sounding the political trumpet.

I could and I may give further explanation of why I say Trump is a man after my own heart. Since the primaries, the politicians and pundits reluctantly admit that Trump's tactics worked for the primaries but will not work for the general election. We shall see. The campaign is just getting started. "You ain't seen nor heard nothin' yet." Trump is a master at communication. He is unique in the history of American politics.

Friday, August 19, 2016 at 9:05am EDT
It's all O.K. now. Republicans, who have been Never Trumpers, need to forgive Donald and come to the Party.

Friday, August 19, 2016 at 3:27pm EDT
They love the Trumpster in Cajun Country. Who cares whether Obama or Hillary visits when one can have a visitation from The Donald? People who lost everything were reaching out just to have their caps autographed by Mr. Trump. Evidently, it has become the responsibility of the President to comfort people in times of natural disasters. Or are these acts of God's judgment? Either way, who wants to be hugged by Obama or Hillary? Yikes!

EXTREME VETTING
Monday, August 22, 2016, Indiana University
Before entering the Kingdom of God, there is an extreme vetting process, which God has established. God just does not let anyone in his Kingdom without a thorough check of his character; he must express true repentance and faith in the Lord Jesus Christ.

Jesus warned in the Sermon on the Mount, *"Not everyone who saith unto me, Lord, Lord shall enter into the Kingdom of heaven; but he that doeth the will of my Father which is in heaven,"--Matt 7:21.*

The immigration officials are letting people in this country who oppose our basic principles as enunciated in our Constitution. Colleges and universities are no longer properly vetting prospective students. There has been a general lowering of standards to receive a college degree. Churches often do not properly vet those who they receive into membership.

We exercised extreme vetting procedures today as we have always done on campus, I said, extreme vetting. Our preaching quickly provokes students to confess to their sins. Regrettably, they confess without shame so they do not qualify to enter the Kingdom. Drunkards, dope fiends, fornicators, sodomites, etc., should not even be allowed to enroll in our universities much less graduate and go and become professionals such as teachers, doctors and lawyers. There should be extreme vetting processes to enter these professions.

We had a consistent audience of 25-35 students throughout the afternoon. Nathan E., a sinner, who has been on my mailing list since the early eighties, came out to hear us today. I had a conversation with him. He tells me his wife is still agitated over my preaching three decades later. I am encouraged that she is still bothered over my words after all these years. Three decades from now people will still be agitated over Trump's call for "extreme vetting." They will never forget the Trumpster!

Thursday, August 25, 2016 at 12:55am EDT
Jed Smock shared Trump Landslide 2016's photo.

Can you believe Hillary's pant suit? How will she get anyone to vote for her? Mr. Trump is always well dressed in a business suit and tie ready to make a deal. Two witches Hillary and Cher. Cher looks a lot better, at least from a distance.

Thursday, August 25, 2016 at 10:24am EDT

Trump is turning the table on the Democrats using tactics they have perfected for decades.

Saturday, August 27, 2016 at 9:01am EDT

Donald Trump is too good of a story for the media to let go. So far Trump has been treated much worse by the press than Ronald Reagan. I suspect that to change. The media will see that it is in their interest that Trump not be defeated. Hillary is a bore; Trump provides great press, like him or not. Trump is a star; Hillary is, well, Hillary is just a tired old. . .

Sunday, August 28, 2016 at 7:53pm EDT

Indeed, Daniel was a man of principle, who advised heathen, idolatrous kings of Babylon and Media-Persia. However, I suspect that many envious Jews perceived Daniel as a man who compromised principle in serving these pagan Kings. Many want to frame the argument that those of us who support Trump are unprincipled. Who is attempting to put a guilt trip on whom? There are principled Christians on both the pro and anti-Trump side.

THE TRUMP TRANSPARENCY
Thursday, September 1, 2016
Purdue University

Bro started the meeting while I parked the car. When I arrived, he had several listening. I was able to build up the crowd a little more. Students were attentive; I wore my "Make America Great Again" cap. It is a good attention getter. I told the students, "I am representing

Donald Trump but the main person I represent is Jesus Christ."

I find it useful to use Trump to bring forth a discussion on Christian ethics. For instance, as Christians can we protect our national borders? Does government have to provide health care for citizens?

A student accused Trump, "He is a hypocrite; he opposes immigration yet his wife is an immigrant."

I corrected the student, "Trump opposes illegal immigration; Melania Trump entered our country legally."

The student protested, "She is a porn star."

I replied, "She was a model who posed naked in youthful indiscretions. She will be the only First Lady whom everyone has had the opportunity to see naked. This goes to show that a Trump presidency will be the most transparent presidency ever. These days a transparent presidency is highly promoted. Certainly, Hillary will never have the opportunity to be so transparent. She would turn everyone away. It is difficult enough looking at her pant suits. What is she hiding under those pant suits anyway?"

I hope my satire is not too bawdy for my FB friends.

I had a lengthy confrontation with a bearded tattooed hairy legged person, who claimed to have been born with female genitalia. The person talked pleasantly. The creature shook my hand when she/he left.

These days it is getting hard to tell what people are unless we see them naked. Apparently, there is doubt in the mind of some as to the gender of Michelle Obama. With Mrs. Trump's transparency, there will be no doubt that the First Lady will actually be a female should her husband be elected. Under Hillary, we won't even have a First Lady. We will have a co-presidency with Bill and her fighting over who is the decider, which may be the best reason not to vote for Hillary.

The last 30 minutes of my session I did have an attentive group as I explained that Christianity is the most reasonable, coherent and believable religion, which gives intelligent answers to the great questions of life concerning origins, meaning, morals and destiny…

Sunday, September 4, 2016 at 11:36pm EDT
Some Pentecostal movement from Mr. Trump?

Monday, September 5, 2016 at 8:32pm EDT
Many FB friends may be too young to remember this woman's *(Phyllis Schlafly)* contribution to the conservative movement. She was more influential than anyone in defeating "the Equal Rights Amendment" to the Constitution. She came out early for Donald Trump.

Monday, September 5, 2016 at 8:50pm EDT
The man of God gives counsel and a gift to the man running for president. Trump's a listener. It seems he has ears to hear. This could prove to be a very significant moment.

Tuesday, September 6, 2016 at 8:02pm EDT
Mrs. Schlafly's last article before her passing. Trump supporters have compared Trump to Reagan and the Never Trump crowd ridicules the comparison. Mrs. S. actually knew both men. Reagan was often commended for his optimism; certainly Mr. Trump has this quality. I don't know anyone among the Never Trump naysayers

who have the conservative credentials of Mrs. S. Like Trump, she was a street fighter.

Friday, September 9, 2016 at 9:55pm EDT
"Phyllis endorsed me at a time when it was not necessarily the thing to do, even the popular thing to do, and I will never forget that that had a great, great impact," Trump added. "I look forward to being with her family tomorrow."

Saturday, September 10, 2016 at 8:51pm EDT
Hillary is simply envious of the passionate and committed following what Trump has, when she has nothing like it.

Sunday, September 11, 2016 at 11:13pm EDT
"I searched for a man among them who would build up the wall and stand in the gap before Me for the land, so that I would not destroy it; but I found no one,"--Ezekiel 22:30.

Has God found such a man in Donald J. Trump? Our country is being destroyed by illegal aliens. Mr. Trump has volunteered to build the wall. Meanwhile, preachers must stand in the gap and rebuild the Moral Law of God or the physical Great Wall of Trump will not save the land.

THE DEPLORABLES
Monday September 12, 2016
University of Illinois
I opened my preaching saying, *"Please allow us to introduce ourselves. We are the people Hillary Clinton calls 'The Deplorables.' We are against Islam and*

homosexuality. We are against such racist programs as affirmative action; ironically, we are therefore regarded as racist. We want to build a wall preventing illegal aliens from entering the country, which Hillary considers xenophobic, even though we welcome legal immigrants. We expect Mexico to pay for the wall, since Mexicans created the problem. We make a distinction between the roles of women and men, which Hillary regards as sexist. We deplore the idea of crooked Hillary in the White House with her Muslim advisors, like Huma. We want to make America great again by turning America back to God."

It was a lively day. After 4 PM I had a group around me of students with sincere questions. Mikhail, Bro, Sister Pat and I left campus at 5:30

Sister Cindy was faithful to return to Missouri State today. Cindy concluded her day saying, *"The Deplorables! That's catchy, Hillary, and after 3 hours at Missouri State University I am feeling rather deplorable! Make America Great Again!"*

Friday, September 16, 2016 at 9:02pm EDT
Trump is a winner!

Friday, September 16, 2016 at 11:38pm EDT
If the Trumpster makes this song his campaign song, he can't be beat. Donald J. Trump beaten by the wicked witch? No way!

Do You Hear the People Sing?

By Michael Maguire

Do you hear the people sing?
Singing the songs of angry men?
It is the music of the people
Who will not be slaves again!
When the beating of your heart
Echoes the beating of the drums
There is a life about to start
When tomorrow comes!

Will you join in our crusade?
Who will be strong and stand with me?
Somewhere beyond the barricade
Is there a world you long to see?

Then join in the fight
That will give you the right to be free!

Do you hear the people sing?
Singing the songs of angry men?
It is the music of the people

Who will not be slaves again!
When the beating of your heart
Echoes the beating of the drums
There is a life about to start
When tomorrow comes!

Will you give all you can give
So that our banner may advance
Some will fall and some will live...

Trump Train is Speeding
Through the Land

Sunday, September 18, 2016 at 10:13pm EDT

The article does not mention this but from what I know about the Hispanic culture I am not sure these people would vote for a female president. Obama, yes, but Hillary is a woman trying to move in what is still largely a man's world. I believe that is a hurdle that she may not overcome, especially among Hispanics. After all, Hillary can't even climb into a van anymore without assistance, let alone jump hurdles. Hispanics tend to be a very personal people; Trump has lots of personality; Hillary is a cold fish. Hispanics are hot blooded.

Thursday, September 22, 2016 at 10:54pm EDT

Wow! Trump's going to get more black votes than any Republican for a long time. The Trump train is speeding through the land. The pastor is amazed at his stamina and so am I. Who can keep up with this 70 year-old man? Hillary can't.

Thursday, September 22, 2016 at 11:31pm EDT

Don King is a big endorsement for Trump. King is a black version of the Trumpster. Move aside Al Sharpton, here comes King to the W.H.

Monday, September 26, 2016 at 9:38am EDT

Tonight's debate is Lisa Simpson vs. Bart. Lisa is the smart and studious one. Bart is the class clown and troublemaker. The moderator is Principal Skinner. Lisa makes her case of calm and liberalism but Bart ends up getting his way by getting all the attention. Humor and fun are what Bart is all about. Bart is unpredictable. Who knows what he might do? Hillary invites Marc Cuban so the Donald *trumps* her by inviting Bill's bimbos and rape victims. Bart is smart and fun; Lisa in the end is boring. Trump might even have a few tricks for Lester Holt.

Monday, September 26, 2016 at 9:45am EDT

The debate might be billed as "the Rumble in the Jungle (Zaire)," when Ali won the heavy weight title from George Foreman with a knock out in the 8th round in 1974. Ali was tactically superior to Forman with his "rope a dope" maneuvers.

The Clinton reign is about to end. The brash, colorful, dancing Trump will be the new Champion. Interestingly, it was an avid Trump supporter, Don King, who was the promoter of the "Fight of the Century." With the help of Don King, some black pastors and other popular black figures, Trump is going to deflect Hillary's haymaker punch, which is the block black vote. This is not a real debate; it is a show. And Donald J. Trump is the master showman.

Monday, September 26, 2016 at 9:20pm EDT

It looks like Hillary is in the foreground and Trump in the background. Her red outfit is a better contrast with the blue background than Trump's suit. Of course, Trump could not wear red.

Monday, September 26, 2016 at 10:39pm EDT
Of course, Hillary doesn't look presidential. We have never had a woman president to which we can compare her. Past presidents all look like and have been men.

Monday, September 26, 2016 at 10:40pm EDT
Neither candidate made any significant mistakes or gaffs in the debate.

Tuesday, September 27, 2016 at 5:13am EDT
Craig Rogers put it best, "Trump did alright considering it was two to one."

Tuesday, September 27, 2016 at 5:31am EDT
As for Hillary looking presidential, her hair style does appear to be similar to early American presidents. I suspect that she, like Washington and others, wears a wig some of the time. Now that red pant suit does not look presidential at all. Previous presidents have worn dark suits. I would say she looks more like John Adams, who was short and stocky and not too well-liked. She is no Washington or Lincoln in stature, which is for sure.

Maybe Hillary could take some sort of hormones and grow a beard. Whoever heard of an American president being called Mrs. President and having a First Man instead of a First Lady? Then there was the silly smile she wore throughout the debate. Portraits of presidents up until Reagan have a taciturn look. Of course, IKE was known for his smile as president, not so much during the war. Does Hillary play golf? Perhaps she should take up the game to be more presidential. Golf seems to be the favorite past time of Presidents since IKE and certainly with Obama. Trump, well he owns golf courses. I like that better than playing the game.

Trump is FUN. Hillary is BORING.

Thursday, September 29, 2016 at 2:41pm EDT

Trump's rallies are fun, fun and more FUN! Hillary is BORING.

Friday, September 30, 2016 at 5:43pm EDT

So the truth is coming out. Hillary made fun of Trump for complaining about the microphone, suggesting that it was just an excuse.

Trump often refers to Patton. The man knew how to pray. Do we have any generals or chaplains who know how to pray?

Tuesday, October 4, 2016 at 8:45pm EDT

Trump is an admirer of Patton; however, The Donald is a softie compared to the General, when it comes to dealing with "PTSD."

Sex and Tax Returns

Friday, October 7, 2016 at 8:25pm EDT

Why should the tape of Trump speaking lewdly of women hurt his campaign? Women have been speaking of themselves in those terms for decades; one of the grosser displays is the theatrical production, "The Vagina Monologues."

I was in a fraternity in college; shamefully this type of talk was common even in the early 60's by boys in regard to girls. Most college boys regard women as a mere piece of _ _ _.

And what is worse, the females are so insecure in their femininity, that they have come to think of themselves as a hunk of meat. Does anyone suppose Kennedy, LBJ and Clinton were any more gentlemanly than Trump?

Sunday, October 9, 2016 at 8:10am EDT

When I was young, I used to hear that when women fall, they fall lower than men. Also, I was told that it was women who civilized the frontier. The two primary civilizing institutions were the church and the school.

Now, the school and feminism are the primary influences in turning this country back to savages. Voting in Hell-Dog Hillary may be the death blow to our nation. She is against borders. The Clintons are both morally bankrupt. At least Trump puts America first and wants to build the wall!

Monday, October 10, 2016 at 12:16am EDT

Trump had much better optics. A few times it seemed he was stalking Hillary. I like the way he paced the stage and at other times stood behind his chair seemingly in thought waiting to pounce on the tigress.

Trump looks and acts like a lion, a very smart one. He was not at all intimated by the moderators, especially the sodomite. No doubt he has been under a lot of pressure the last few days but it did not affect him. It was a brilliant move appearing with Clinton's rape victims just before the debate. The media fell into a trap. Trump outmaneuvered Hillary.

THE TRUMP HOOK
Monday, October 10, 2016
Northwestern University

Northwestern is a private campus so we stayed on the public sidewalk at the entrance gate. There was plenty of pedestrian traffic. However, it did take a while to gather an audience.

My hook was Donald J. Trump. I proclaimed, "We represent evangelicals for Donald J. Trump," I wore my Trump cap, which says, "Make America Great Again."

Regrettably, students have been taught that America was never great, starting with Columbus, who was a murderer and racist. They cite slavery, segregation and the treatment of Native Americans, suppression of women, etc. As for Trump, I said any of his moral shortcomings will be filled by the strong Christian and morally upright, Mike Pence as V.P.

A student stole my Trump hat and ran off with it. Even though many witnessed the incident, no one expressed their disapproval. Actually, students hate Jesus even more than they hate Trump.

When I announced that earlier a student stole my Trump hat, many in the crowd clapped, which is typical for liberals, who do not respect private property, especially property of those who are not P.C.

Thursday, October 13, 2016 at 10:37pm EDT

Even if all the allegations against Trump are true, Anderson Cooper's sins are worse.

Friday, October 14, 2016 at 9:39am EDT

During the primaries both CNN and Fox gave extensive coverage to Trump's rallies. In the general election, he is merely getting clips of these events, even on Fox. There has been a significant shift on Fox News since the forced departure of Roger Ailes, partly on account of accusations from Megyn Kelly. Trump had her number from the beginning. Trump's rallies give people reason to vote for him. Hillary's comparatively few public appearances are always boring.

Friday, October 14, 2016 at 11:13am EDT
From my wife: *"Mom, would you vote for Trump if he groped me?"*
One of my five daughters almost stumped me with this question this morning.
My reply, "I would rather you be groped by Trump, than raped and murdered by an illegal criminal who crossed the southern border or have your legs bombed off and blinded by an ISIS radical!" This is serious folks!!! Getting the vote out for Trump 2016!!

Saturday, October 15, 2016 at 7:37am EDT
The reason Mr. Trump does not release his Federal Income Tax forms is that he would be embarrassed for the American people to know what a generous man he truly is. He must have made extremely large deductible charitable contributions. If people knew how magnanimous the man actually is, he would lose his reputation as hard core businessman. Also, he would lose his rewards in Heaven--if he makes it.

Saturday, October 15, 2016 at 4:13pm EDT
Let's face it, liberals and Democrats do not really care about Trump's sex talk and alleged advances on women, even if the worst is true. They glorify sexual immorality.

They just don't like Trump's stand on the issues and the threat that he represents to their power.

On the other hand, the main concern of conservatives and Republicans is not Bill's lustful behavior with women and Hillary's enabling. Their concern is the Clinton's liberal, socialistic and globalist agenda. The whole sex controversy is a smokescreen. Right now the left seems to be doing most of the smoking. Hopefully, voters on Election Day can see through all the fumes.

Monday, October 17, 2016 at 9:27pm EDT

Mrs. Trump is defending her husband today. Melania needs to get out on the campaign trail with The Donald. She is poised, articulate and convincing. Obviously no bimbo! She's a 9. She would get a 10 without the indiscretions of her youth. But then she was a model.

Monday, October 17, 2016 at 11:14pm EDT

Trump the Brawler, he is just what the Republicans need; he is what our country needs. Donald J. Trump is our champion; he is our Samson.

Tuesday, October 18, 2016 at 8:58am EDT

It is understandable that Trump objects to the Saturday Night Live spoof on the debate. To this day there are many people who believe that Sarah Palin actually said, "You can see Russia from my house." Often these funny skits can have more influence on the electorate than the actual debates.

On SNL, Hillary is played by a pretty and young comedian, when in fact Hillary has never been particularly attractive and she is certainly no longer young. Why are these comedy clips replayed over news programs even before they become news? Of course, the answer is to influence the voters to regard Trump negatively.

"Politics is a dirty job and tonight may the best MAN win."--Ruben Israel

Wednesday, October 19, 2016 at 10:31pm EDT
The main story to come out of tonight's debate will be Trump's answer about accepting the results of the election.

Friday, October 21, 2016 at 11:23am EDT
I like the open animosity between Trump and Hillary; the Bushes and Clintons have been and remain too cozy. The stakes are too high in this election to be friendly.

The battle lines are being drawn.

ROLL OVER DONALD, MY WIFE IS A TEN
Friday, October 21, 2016,
University of Nebraska
Cindy had to compete with a well-promoted *Black Lives Matter* rally to capture the attention of the students. Hundreds of guilt laden white liberals gathered to bow at the feet of the black racists, who had obviously subdued their rhetoric for their targeted college-educated white audience. These were mostly sons and daughters of the sixties generation who gathered with students. These people are ashamed of their "white privilege." I know liberals well; I was one of them back in the sixties; I have been confronting them since my conversion 44 years ago.

Cindy lost much of her initial audience, when the BLM rally started a 12:30, but gradually rebuilt it as students became bored with the racist rhetoric. After all, they have been brainwashed with it all their lives. Sister Cindy said, "The problem in the African-American community is that the men have shirked their responsibly in the home."

I know of no preacher, who perseveres more to gather an audience than Cindy. And she enjoys every moment. She deserves a ten rating. If I had been alone, I probably would have waited until the BLM rally was over.

By the time Cindy turned the crowd over to me the BLM meeting was ended and we had a large audience, which became increasingly rowdy. I was in my best form belittling every politically correct thought and pulling my trigger against every "trigger warning" which might offend those who perceive themselves as victims of "racism, sexism, classism," and all the other isms. Sadly, liberals suffer from the mental disorder.

Of course, there are few things which trigger me more than feminism. The females have lost their femininity and the males have lost their masculinity to the diabolical movement called feminism. The leading idol and advocate of feminism is now running for president. Women have lost all sense of true womanhood and motherly instinct, when they will promote murder of the fruit of their own womb.

There was a black student, who was a member of my college fraternity, Delta Upsilon. I triggered him when I commended our fraternity for opening up membership to black men. Thankfully, we still haven't rushed any women, as yet. I triggered a "Native American," when I said, "Thankfully, Columbus introduced the savages to Christian Civilization." They are referred to as savages as late as 1776 in our most sacred document, *The Declaration of Independence*. I pointed out that the term

Native American is a European term. The original residents of what we call America referred to themselves by their tribe, not as Native Americans.

I was speaking to a generation who has become dependent on a government dominated by Democrats. Democrats want to keep blacks on the government plantation. On the other hand, Donald J. Trump promises to set "African Americans" free to be full participants in the American dream, through jobs, instead of encouraging another generation to be on the public dole.

As I smashed one after another of their politically correct idols, the audience went into an emotional rampage. I must say that I enjoyed every moment of the conflict. Yes, I did present the gospel.

During my long idol-destroying session, Sister Cindy was doing effective personal ministry on the sidelines with a young man named Drew, who had contemplated suicide. He was in Cindy's initial audience. A month ago his long-time sexual relationship had ended, when the girl left. He asked her, "What is wrong with having sex before marriage with someone you love?" Cindy spent over an hour answering his questions. He countered many of her answers; nevertheless, after their long talk, Cindy asked him, "On a scale of one to ten, how well have I answered your questions?" Drew replied, "I give you a ten, definitely a ten."

Sunday, October 23, 2016 at 10:27am EDT
I notice the media is misrepresenting Trump again. They speak of his refusal to accept the election results in the last debate. This is what he actually said, "I will look at it at the time. I'm not looking at anything now. I'll

look at it at the time." This is significant. He merely refused to say if he would accept the results or not.

Monday, October 24, 2016 at 2:09pm EDT

Can Trump somehow tie Clinton to her hometown Cubs and use that to get Cleveland/Ohio support?

Monday, October 24, 2016 at 10:54pm EDT

I will enthusiastically and without reservation cast my vote on November 8 for Donald J. Trump. I do not get the evangelical leaders, who are reluctantly wringing their hands in finally siding with Trump. Trump has a good plan in his Gettysburg Address in which he outlines his Contract with America. His appointment of the strong and mature Christian conservative, Mike Pence, should have convinced these ministers. Trump is committed to appointing pro-life judges to the High Court. What more do these people want?

As for Trump's Christianity, he is as much saved, if not more so, than these evangelical leaders, who are in such distress concerning casting a vote for The Donald. All the sexual accusations that I have read about are at least a decade old. Just consider the alternative, which is enough to settle it in the mind of any reasonable man.

STUMPING FOR TRUMP AND JESUS
Tuesday, October 25, 2016
Colorado State University

This campus has a literal tree stump in the center of the mall designated for free speech. Nasty women for Hillary had a table set up next to the stump giving out fresh baked cookies. I introduced myself as representing Evangelicals for Donald J. Trump. The Hillary campaigner was a gray and short haired female, who reminded me of the gal who accused Trump of being all over her on the airplane. Liberal women have that certain look.

One male got so mad at me that he smashed some of the feminists' bake goods, erroneously thinking I was giving out the cookies. How he got this idea, I know not; my wife was not even with me today. No doubt, if some Trump supporter had broken the cookies, he would have been arrested. But the feminists were not disturbed about the cookies being crumbled by one of their own.

Males today remind me of crumbled cookies before the feminists. The males are afraid that if they don't go along with the feminists' agenda, they will be cut off.

A female student defined love as accepting anybody for whom or what they are. I asked, "Would you accept a rapist?" Well, I triggered her; she burst into tears acknowledging that she had been raped three years ago. Later, she apologized and we had a civil conversation while Sister Pat was preaching. The student admitted that she had sex with her boyfriend, who was now deployed. Also, she admitted that she had conceived out of wedlock and had put the baby up for adoption. I gave her credit for not aborting the baby.

Meanwhile, another "Christian" girl had joined us, who admitted she and her "Christian boyfriend" were having sex. I informed her that he was her boy enemy. A boyfriend would encourage his girlfriend to a life of virtue.

The last hour we had mostly a stage-five with Sister Pat holding forth to a group of eight. Matthew Murray, a local street preacher, witnessed on the sidelines. There were a number of vocal Trump supporters, including some girls.

Tuesday, October 25, 2016 at 9:34pm EDT

Make sure to watch the fire between the catty, Megyn Kelly and Newt Gingrich. Trump had Megyn's number from the first debate among the Republicans.

Wednesday, October 26, 2016 at 12:21pm EDT

Women, women, women everywhere on TV news telling us what to think or what women think, especially these blonds on Fox sticking their bare legs in everyone's face. There are a few brilliant ones like Laura Ingram and Judge Jeanine. But the Judge needs to put on her judicial robes when she is on TV to cover herself up. It doesn't take me long to tune them out.

If Hillary is elected, it will get even worse. Oh, for the days when there was just Cronkite, Huntley and Brinkley and Reynolds. Wait, they were all libs. At least Barbara Walters has pretty much disappeared. She slept her way to her position. I have never watched the View, which would be worse than waterboarding.

Thursday, October 27, 2016 at 1:52am EDT

This is Trump at his inspirational best; he has the faith and experience to rebuild and revitalize America. If you want to know what Trump is all about, then watch this 10-minute speech. As a side, he commends Newt for putting Megyn Kelly in her place last night (my words, not Trump's).

Thursday, October 27, 2016 at 11:34am EDT

Donald Trump does not drink; we need a sober man in the White House; maybe Hillary's stumbling has nothing to do with Parkinson's Disease.

Thursday, October 27, 2016 at 12:02pm EDT

In the world of sports they say it is a big mistake for a team that is winning to be less aggressive in closing out a game. One should not concentrate on protecting a lead but increasing the lead and pounding one's opposition. Hillary has been running a non-aggressive campaign; whereas Trump is tirelessly campaigning and remaining on the offensive.

Hillary's campaign is lackluster at best. Perhaps it is the only strategy for her, since even her supporters agree she is not a people-person or a good campaigner, like her husband. Trump is active all the day, rallying at night and tweeting before dawn. When does this man sleep? Have a drink, Hillary, and go back to bed! Maybe she is confident that it is all rigged? Soon we shall see.

Thursday, October 27, 2016 at 12:24pm EDT

If Trump wins, this will be the most historical election in U.S. history. Unless one is a racist or feminist, a female becoming president is insignificant. But for an outsider, like Trump, who took on the establishment of his own party, and is a businessman, to become president, this is historical. It will be the most studied election in our history.

If Hillary is elected, we will see the same old tired and stupid liberal smirks, which we have had to put up with over the last 30 years.

What will a Trump administration look like? He will bring smart men with a vision to Washington, men of accomplishment, and some bright women, too. Of course, he will have to give some important offices to loyal old pols (politicians) like Gingrich and Rudy G. They are deserving for standing with him when so few prominent Republicans have.

Friday, October 28, 2016 at 9:21pm EDT

"It might not be as rigged as I thought."--Classic Trump.

Sunday, October 30, 2016 at 8:04pm EDT

"We never thought we would say thank you to Anthony Wiener"--Classic Trump.

Monday, October 31, 2016 at 8:28pm EDT

Mr. Donald J. Trump is taking upon himself the arrows fired towards us by our diabolical enemies. He knew this when he entered on his mission. Be a part of the movement. All aboard the Trump train that is going aboard! Be a part of a pivot point in history. They say Mr. Trump does not know how to pivot. November 8 will prove them wrong!

Tuesday, November 1, 2016 at 9:58am EDT

The Never Trump peoples' favorite candidates were usually Ben Carson or Ted Cruz who were promoted as men of principle. Both of them have boarded the Trump train, Carson boarded early. The moderate Republicans, like the Bushes and the Ohio Governor, are still sitting at the station. I urge my Never Trump friends to follow those whom you promoted as principled men and board the Trump diesel now. Help derail Hillary, while we still can.

Tuesday, November 1, 2016 at 10:21am EDT

Donald J. Trump is fondly known as the Orange Man. He's going down to Florida to get some votes in his shoes. "She's the fastest train on the line. It's that Orange Blossom Special rollin' down the seaboard line."

Wednesday, November 2, 2016 at 6:35pm EDT

Hysterical Hillary, can you stand to hear this for the next four years? Shut her up! Vote Trump/Pence!

Wednesday, November 2, 2016 at 11:08pm EDT

"She is so much better qualified than the other guy." Hey, Obama, Trump is the guy. Hillary is the gal. Real men don't want the gal. Don't try to make a metrosexual out of us guys. American men are waking up and there is going to be a backlash against feminism. Donald J. Trump wants to put Hillary in her place, which should be jail.

Make America Great Again

Thursday, November 3, 2016 at 10:20am EDT

The last time the Cubs won the World Series, America was at the height of the Progressive Era and Teddie Roosevelt was president. The Progressive Era turned into the New Deal and modern liberalism (socialism). Hopefully, the Cubs win marks the end of this long miserable time in our history, which has weakened the American Spirit. May the Cubs epic victory pave the way for the triumph of Donald J. Trump.

May Mr. Trump bring about a return to the Gilded Age of American history and a robust renewal of the American Spirit of business and industrial progress, as opposed to social programs, feminism and white guilt. We do not need more reform; we need a rebirth of the vision that our Founding Fathers had for our Republic (not democracy).

Make America Great Again; elect Donald J. Trump president.

Thursday, November 3, 2016 at 2:45pm EDT

Melania Trump for First Lady! Donald's ace in the hole! The Melania card should put him over the top.

Thursday, November 3, 2016 at 5:12pm EDT

I very much enjoy Trump's sense of humor as he promised to stay nice and cool and stay on point. I don't think that was scripted. Hillary has no sense of humor and is boring.

Friday, November 4, 2016, Miami University, Oxford, OH

As we drove through rural SW Ohio, we saw a multitude of TRUMP/PENCE yard signs. Cindy saw one Hillary sign. A number of students said they were voting for Trump. Hopefully, this is an omen that Trump will carry Ohio on Tuesday.

Donald J. Trump, the Loveable Rogue
Friday November 4, 2016

Part of Donald J. Trump's appeal is that he is considered by some as a loveable rogue. Loveable rogues are often portrayed in fiction. The standard for loveable rogues is Rhett Butler in "Gone with the Wind." Clint Eastwood in his Westerns is usually portrayed as a loveable rogue. Many of us have known loveable rogues either in our family or circle of acquaintances. Robin Hood of folklore may be thought of as a loveable rogue.

The lovable rogue attempts to "beat the system" and improve himself, not by ordinary or widely accepted means. Lovable rogues are not paragons of virtue because they often seem to act for their own personal profit; however, they are charming or sympathetic enough to convince others to cheer for them. Although they appear at first to act only for personal gain, lovable rogues justify their actions according to some unknown ethical motivation or, at least, demonstrate the capacity to atone for their wrongdoings. They maintain a flexible code of ethics.

The lovable rogue's rough temperament is viewed not as repulsive and alarming so much as exciting and adventurous. He is generally regarded as handsome or attractive, especially to women, and his daredevil attitude further makes him striking. He often has a fiery temperament and is streetwise, possessing practical knowledge, as opposed to formal education.

"Despite his common external appearance of selfishness, foolhardiness, or emotional detachment, the lovable rogue may in fact strongly associate with a highly idealistic belief system and understand the concept of a code of honor so highly valued that it transcends normal social constraints, such as conformity, tradition, or the law. This sense of an internalized, personal code is usually what makes the lovable rogue lovable, since it serves to confirm that he is moral, whereas he may have appeared at first glance to be immoral.

The lovable rogue, thus, is not a villain, because he has either a sincere, strong sense of morality (though he may be unwilling to expose it) or has the definite potential for establishing such a moral sense. In addition, his tendency to violate norms may be regarded as a positive trait—having a highly individualistic, creative, or self-reliant personality."

[The above description of the loveable rogue is adapted from an article in Wikipedia].

Loveable rogues should not be confused with just plain rogues like Hillary Clinton. She is usually acknowledged, even by her supporters, as not a people-person or someone with a likeable personality. Her husband, Bill, may pass for at least a likeable rogue.

Saturday, November 5, 2016 at 1:41pm EDT

Trump told a crowd in the town of Hershey, PA, "I'm here all by myself... No guitar, no piano, no nothing." This is one reason open-air preachers identify with Trump. We just rely on the Truth to draw the multitudes…no advanced publicity, no Gospel music, nothing but the BIBLE and the Holy Ghost.

Saturday, November 5, 2016 at 5:13pm EDT

Only our Trumpster could pull this one off. I could not have. Certainly, Hillary could not. Trump sees the baby as a future construction worker. Hillary wants to continue to allow women to murder their babies. If Hillary saw the baby she would probably see it as a future rapper. Rappers are all about destructing our culture. Trump and his progeny are about building.

It was risky of Trump to take the baby in his arms. What if the baby had cried? This is a symbolic picture of the Trump candidacy and presidency.

Every father and mother should vote for Trump, the Lion King!

Saturday, November 5, 2016 at 6:24pm EDT

I notice today Hillary is losing her voice already. Trump has five stops scheduled for this day. He usually speaks about an hour each time. He sounds as strong as ever. The Bible does say that the woman is "the weaker vessel." Why choose the weaker, when you can have the stronger? Vote for the Lion King, Donald J. Trump.

Monday, November 7, 2016 at 7:27pm EST

In John 18, we behold the tragic spectacle of the rulers of the chosen people leading their promised Messiah to the Gentile ruler, Pilate, to be put to death and thereby forfeiting their place in the Kingdom of God and their national existence. America is a chosen nation. Our Pilgrim Fathers saw it as a shining city upon a hill, the New Jerusalem!

In this 2016 election, there are Republican leaders, professing Christians, like the Bushes and other Never Trump conservatives and evangelical Christians, who may vote for Hillary. Hillary supports open borders. A nation cannot exist without borders. She promotes murder of our progeny.

Trump advocates enforcing our immigration laws, promotes life and is determined to take our country from the grip of the internationalists and put it back into the hands of the American people.

Pilate allowed the people to vote as to whom he would release, Jesus of Nazareth, the King of the Jews, or Barabbas? The multitudes made the fatal choice of the wrong man, Barabbas, who was a robber. Who will the American people choose on Election Day, Mr. Trump, who has promised to protect the Church, or the traitorous thief, Hillary?

When the multitudes cried, "Crucify Jesus," Pilate said, *"I am innocent of this man's blood. It is your responsibility!"*—Matt 27:24.

Pilate reminds me of those who will not vote for Hillary but will cast their vote for someone who has no chance of winning, thus making it more likely that Hillary will capture the White House. Politics is a dirty business. Never Trumpers refuse to fight. Trump has been willing to get down and dirty with Hillary. More power to him. Take back the White House; take back America. The battle is the Lord's.

Tuesday, November 8, 2016 at 11:30pm EST
Fox gives Wisconsin to Trump!

Wednesday, November 9, 2016 at 3:12am EST
Mr. Trump will be a great president. He is a great man.

Wednesday, November 9, 2016 at 3:43am EST
I just turned off the TV; virtually all the pundits were wrong and most of them still don't get it. They ought to be fired.

Chapter 3

President Elect

"From this day forward, a new vision will govern our land. From this day forward, it's going to be only America first, America first," President *Trump, Inaugural Address 2017.*

A Joyous Day

Wednesday, November 9, 2016 at 6:00 am EST
Post from my wife: *"The Wicked Witch is dead!!!!"*

Wednesday, November 9, 2016 at 7:47am EST
Kellyanne Conway is the woman of the hour, not Hillary. Kellyanne is a self-made woman; Hillary never was. She was made by her husband and then by the Democratic machine.

Thursday, November 10, 2016 at 5:55pm EST
Dinner party at Smock's celebrating with Glenn Pirates *(my High School friends)* Trump's election!

Friday November 11, 2016 at 7:05am EST
http://www.jconline.com/story/news/college/2016/11/10/purdue-students-rally-against-preachers-celebrating-trump/93608078/

Friday, November 11, 2016 at 7:29am EST
What a joyous day that will be, when we hear Donald J. Trump take the oath of office.

Friday, November 11, 2016 at 9:12pm EST
In this sign (cross) you will conquer and Make America Great Again, President Elect, Donald J. Trump.

Saturday, November 12, 2016 at 10:31am EST
The black spokesmen that Trump inspired made a difference in this election; the most notable was Ben Carson, but there were others less known, which may have even had a greater impact than Carson.

Trump said a few months ago, that after four years he will have 95% of the African-Americans voting for him. And you know what? It would not surprise me at all.

Saturday, November 12, 2016 at 7:12pm EST
How do the media pundits have any credibility at all left? Mr. Trump was right about everything he did, including getting "off message" at times, as well as the little feuds he got involved in with the Muslim guy and Miss Universe (Miss Piggy).

On the other hand, the pundits, who thought they knew so much better than Trump, were wrong about everything concerning Trump and his campaign. Now they are pontificating on what Trump ought to be doing in the transition and his first 100 days in office. They need to shut up and watch Trump. They may learn something from the man, who even Jeb Bush admitted early on has great political instincts.

His "off message" times and feuds just added to the Trump mystic and endeared him to his supporters and kept the attention upon him as he daily won over the electorate with his winsome ways. Trump was ahead all the time. The polls were wrong all along in the general election.

Saturday, November 12, 2016 at 11:23pm EST
Judge Jeanine gives an emotional opening statement celebrating Trump's victory. She stood with Trump all the way.

Sunday, November 13, 2016 at 8:09pm EST
Just finished watching Leslie Stahl's 60 Minutes interview with President Elect Trump. Stahl is older than

I am; it is time that she retires. She asked Trump if he was afraid or intimidated concerning becoming president. Of course, Trump flatly said, "No." I liked it when he said he would not be taking vacations; there is too much work to be done. Seemed like Obama took several vacations a year. Trump is the work horse. Stahl wears far too much lipstick.

Sunday, November 13, 2016 at 8:37pm EST

I want to thank my FB friends who stood steadfastly for Trump. I found your posts encouraging and informative throughout the campaign. I thought about naming names, but I feared that I would leave someone out.

I liked Trump from the beginning, when he was so politically incorrect in what he said about many of the Mexicans, who were crossing the border illegally. Soon with me, it got down to Cruz vs. Trump. I made my decision when I cast my vote for Trump in the Indiana primary after attending an energetic Trump rally in Indianapolis. I was confident that Trump was more likely to defeat Hillary. As I put it then, Trump would be willing to get down and dirty with Hillary.

Sunday, November 13, 2016 at 8:56pm EST

I am sorry that Phyllis Schlafly did not live to see Trump elected. Her early endorsement of Trump encouraged me in backing him. She fought all of her political life against "the Kingpins." I suppose she is looking down from heaven with her usual bright smile. Actually, she is probably laughing heartily at the liberals, whom she outmaneuvered by virtually single-handily defeating the Equal Rights Amendment.

IN THE WAKE OF A PROTEST
Monday, November 14, 2016
Eastern Illinois University

On the steps in front of where we preach, chalk marks remained from a recent anti-Trump rally. The most prominent slogan was, NOT MY PRESIDENT. However, someone had marked a big X though the NOT. Other sayings included, QUEER WITH FEAR and GAY AND SCARED. Also, BLACK LIVES MATTER was chalked on many steps in addition to MUSLIM LIVES MATTER, etc.

Mikhail talked about Trump's victory and he soon gathered several of his groupies, including Cory, who has visited in our home, and who is now pregnant and planning on marrying the father. Evidently, students settled down since the protest. They were generally in good humor today. We never had more than 20 listening on the steps; a good number of which were attentive. Mikhail is very popular on this campus. He always had a small group surrounding him.

There was a core group of about 10, who stayed with us most of the afternoon. The GLBT un-naturals need not be fearful since Trump has said that he considers same-sex marriage as settled law and is expected to pick the first openly gay person to a cabinet position. We proclaimed the gospel of Jesus Christ.

Thursday, November 17, 2016 at 4:09pm EST

Rush gave the one key word that in my opinion sums up the character of Donald J. Trump, "indefatigable." The man's energy and perseverance is amazing, especially considering he is 71 years old. He simply outran Hillary in every way. He also outran much younger Republicans, who were trying to get the nomination. They could just not keep up with The Donald.

Rush says Trump gets up in the morning at 5 AM and sleeps for only four hours each night. He never looks or acts tired. Washington has never seen the likes of our President Elect of whom we can all be proud.

Friday, November 18, 2016 at 10:56pm EST

I just finished watching *"Objectified Trump"* broadcasted on Fox News, an up and personal piece on Donald. He repeatedly gave credit to his parents for his success. I appreciate that. Rush Limbaugh also is careful to give credit to his parents for him becoming so smart. Honor our parents and we are promised a long life. Donald's father, Fred Trump, lived to be 94.

Saturday, November 19, 2016 at 12:32pm EST

To my FB friends, who opposed Trump, remember that this great country is bigger than the President. Bide your time and go about your business. The political tides have their way of shifting. Concentrate on God, family and friends and you can still have a happy and fulfilling life for the next 4 years, then you will have another opportunity to get your man in office.

Saturday, November 19, 2016 at 6:45pm EST

A turning point during the nomination process was Jerry Lewis' endorsement of Trump. Lewis said that Trump was a winner because he was the consummate showman. Lewis felt we needed a showman in the White House. Lewis is to be respected; he has endured through lots of challenges and setbacks. He is somewhat of a philanthropist, although I never much cared for his slapstick humor. Nor do I usually pay that much attention to celebrities. For instance, I have never seen the show, "The Apprentice." But I do think Lewis is one of Hollywood's good guys.

Sunday, November 20, 2016 at 6:10pm EST
I see on Fox that some tattoo artist in N.J. is offering free Trump tattoos. Should I? Perhaps I could relate to students better if I had a tattoo. Also, there is someone else, who has started an organization, *Bikers for Trump.* Should I buy a bike? I guess I am getting carried away.

Monday, November 21, 2016 at 7:25pm EST
Spiro Agnew was weak compared to Donald Trump when it comes to fighting the mainstream media. Washington has never seen the likes of Donald J. Trump. It is going to be an exciting cruise on the Ship of State with Captain Trump at the helm. Never a dull moment…

Wednesday, November 23, 2016 at 9:20pm EST
These policemen getting murdered in cold blood is very disturbing. I put a lot of blame on Obama and his Justice Dept. They are sympathetic to radical groups like Black Lives Matter. Things should change under Trump and Sessions. Law and order will prevail again. We will soon rid ourselves of the community organizer. Thank you, Donald J. Trump, for preparing to drive the rascal out of the White House. We are with you all the way, Mr. Trump.

Thursday, November 24, 2016 at 12:50pm EST

Does anyone think for a moment Trump would have cried if he lost?

Wednesday, November 30, 2016 at 3:25pm EST

Are any of my friends planning on attending the Inauguration of Donald J. Trump? If so, are you hoping to get tickets to any of the events? It should be a day to remember.

Thursday, December 1, 2016 at 11:12pm EST

Pocahontas (Warren) is another one. Are the Democrats going to continue to throw her face at us? Go ahead! Trump has awakened the great sleeping giant, the American workingmen and businessmen, who are tired of the likes of Warren and Pelosi. Productive people can't stand them and others who are constantly playing racial politics.

It's over! The Dems need some new faces. And Chuck Schumer is not one of them, if they expect to regain the confidence of the people that matter and make a difference in this country. Working people and businessmen will make America great again, now that they have been loosed by the man, Trump. And Pence is beside him all the way. Pence was a brilliant choice for VP.

Friday, December 2, 2016 at 12:25am EST

I watched Trump's Cincinnati rally tonight, same Trump who campaigned in Ohio. So much fun watching the people sitting behind Trump; they loved every moment.

There was even a baby being held by her mother. Parents will remind that baby that she attended a Trump rally. One of the best memories in my life will be attending a Trump Rally in Indianapolis during the primaries. The whole Trump phenomenon is as if a dream comes true. The Trump train keeps picking up speed!

Saturday, December 3, 2016 at 7:37am EST
Initially, I wondered why Mr. Trump chose *"You Can't Always Get What You Want"* as his theme song at his rallies and even at the Republican convention. On Election Day, we found that the song proved to be prophetic. For those who are not yet on the Trump train, "if you will give him a try some time, you just might find, you will get what you need."
Oh, the wisdom and humor of President Elect Donald J. Trump!

Melania is Unflappable

Sunday, December 4, 2016 at 11:08pm EST
Melania Trump is unflappable, a perfect fit for her confrontational husband. She should be an outstanding first lady. Despite her revealing modeling in her youth, she seems in all other respects a traditional woman, at least in the European sense. She is the female counterpart to Arnold Schwarzenegger. Both came to America and experienced the American dream by promoting their bodies. One thing, she won't be interfering in the affairs of state.

Tuesday, December 6, 2016 at 7:47pm EST
Isn't it interesting that Bob Dole organized the call between Trump and the President of Taiwan? Dole was on the Trump train from at least the time he won the nomination; it speaks well of him. My respect for Dole has risen but my regard for Romney and the Bushes has fallen. I suppose Dole is too old to serve in the Trump administration, except perhaps in an advisory capacity.

Tuesday, December 6, 2016 at 8:02pm EST
Live coverage of Trump rally in North Carolina on CNN and Fox. He will introduce the Mad Dog tonight. Anything can happen at a Trump rally.

Wednesday, December 7, 2016 at 11:25am EST
Trump should have been Person of the Year in 2015 also. Time used to use the name Man of the Year. Maybe they need to name both a Man and Woman of the Year. Who would you chose as woman of the Year? How about Kellyanne Conway for managing the Trump campaign so effectively? Certainly Hillary does not qualify except as loser of the year.

Thursday, December 8, 2016 at 8:27pm EST
They love Trump in Iowa. He is on live on CNN and Fox.

Friday, December 9, 2016 at 8:08pm EST
Trump is really on his game tonight. Turn on your TV.

Monday, December 12, 2016 at 9:22pm EST
One of the biggest myths during both the primaries and general election was that Trump did not have a ground

game. The fact is he had the strongest ground game, the biggest part of which was his massive rallies, which the pundits pooh pooed.

His 1 AM rally in Michigan on Election Day may have made the difference in that Rust Belt state. To go to MI was a decision made in the last hours of Election Eve. Thirty-one thousand showed up in the middle of the night. Where did they come from at that hour with virtually no time to publicize? God must have brought them, nothing short of a miracle.

Tuesday, December 13, 2016 at 9:22pm EST
Trump replayed Election Night at his thank you rally in Wisconsin. I have heard him do this several times now. Each time is exciting. Trump spoke well of Paul Ryan; they are going to work together to Make America Great Again.

Wednesday, December 14, 2016 at 2:41pm EST
I have made this observation before, but Donald Trump's energy never ceases to amaze me. Yesterday, he spent the day interviewing various important people. Then he flies from NY to Wisconsin for one of his Thank You Rallies. Today, he is back in NY interviewing. He seems to be awake all hours of the night tweeting. Plus, he doesn't care about vacations.

His is going to be a whirlwind presidency, unlike anything America or perhaps the world has ever seen. The man is motivated more than anyone I have ever heard or known. A president with his work ethic is just what America needs.

Hillary could never have kept Trump's pace. She certainly did not during her campaign. She was raising money while he was spending money, much of it his own. The man evidently believes there is no better investment than to invest in himself.

Thursday, December 15, 2016 at 8:25pm EST

Norman Vincent Peale may be looking down from heaven very proud of his disciple, Donald J. Trump.

Saturday, December 17, 2016 at 1:14pm EST

"Trump's roster of agency heads and advisers conspicuously lacks intellectuals, lawyers, and academics of the sort sought by some past presidents. In their place are titans of business and finance from the likes of Exxon Mobil and Goldman Sachs and no fewer than three retired generals in key positions."

Friday, December 23, 2016 at 11:26am EST

Professionally, I am trained as a historian. When I was converted to Christianity, I became an advocate of Divine Providence as the primary mover (not determiner, but guider) of history. In Biblical history, God used great men to accomplish his will, such as Noah, Abraham, Moses, David and the prophets. In the NT, he worked through Jesus and the Apostles.

In the 19th Century, Scottish author, Thomas Carlyle, popularized, *"The Great Man theory to which history can be largely explained by the impact of 'great men' or heroes; highly influential individuals who, due to their personal charisma, intelligence, wisdom, or political skill, utilized their power in a way that had a decisive historical impact."* (Wikipedia)

Could Donald Trump be the highly influential man whom God has raised up to accomplish his will of

Making America Great Again? Even Trump's detractors would have to acknowledge his uncanny political instincts and charisma. He is in a historical position to have the impact of a Washington or Lincoln on U.S. and even world history.

Friday, December 23, 2016 at 9:46pm EST
Good for Trump. Who needs these celebrities? There are many nationally unknown musicians who have talent equal to if not superior to the celebrities, who would consider it an honor to play at the Inauguration. Many of the celebrities, like Elton John, are utterly depraved reprobates. Besides, John is a Brit, we should have Americans playing at the Inauguration.

Thursday, December 29, 2016 at 7:35pm EST
The lame duck in the White House is getting desperate; he knows his goose is cooked as of Jan. 20. President Trump is going to eat his LEGacy for dinner. Then throw the bones to the dogs.

Saturday, December 31, 2016 at 7:14pm EST
I was talking to a businessman friend of mine, Bob Allen. He considers Kellyanne Conway to be the most astute businesswoman he has encountered. He says bureaucrats will be Trump's biggest enemies; they hate entrepreneurs. Every businessman I have met likes Trump.

Make the Church Great Again

Sunday, January 1, 2017 at 7:43am EST

Trump wants to make the church great again by giving it back its voice to speak on political topics. He recognizes the power of Christianity more than some pastors and reiterated this point numerous times in 2016.

Trump is a man of business and action. He has pledged to listen to the voice of the church. Mike Pence can be the moral influence and prayer warrior to support Trump's challenge to return the church to its former glory. The church is the foundation of a strong and great nation. For America to be great again; the church must become even greater, especially in the moral realm.

Tuesday, January 3, 2017 at 10:02pm EST

I see that some Christians are already complaining about the ministers that Trump has invited to his inauguration. As for me, I am pleased that they have been invited and that they will be praying for the new administration. Personally, I plan to join my prayers with their prayers for the health and success of our new President.

Apparently, Paula White's prayer for Trump was answered in Sept. 2015; I look forward to hearing her Inaugural prayer.

Wednesday, January 4, 2017 at 7:19pm EST

"Jed, Happy and blessed Birthday to you. You are older than The Donald and still going strong. Your perseverance inspires younger men like me to labor on. God's blessings to you, my brother."

Sunday, January 8, 2017 at 4:42pm EST

"When you have to deal with a beast, you have to treat him as a beast. It is most regrettable but nevertheless true," said US President Harry S Truman, August 11, 1945, in a letter justifying his decision to drop the atomic bomb on the Japanese cities of Hiroshima and Nagasaki.

Islam is the beast that needs to be vanquished in our generation. Let us pray that President Trump takes on the beast. I like O'Reilly's use of the word, "vanquished," which means totally subdue. Yes, it was regrettable that there was primarily collateral damage in dropping the atom bomb but it was necessary to bring about the unconditional surrender of Japan, which Truman demanded. In order to vanquish WWII Japan, we had to terrorize the Japs with the bomb.

Is there anyone in the Democratic Party who comes anywhere near being the leader that Truman was? We shall see if our Republican president can rise to the occasion. When have we heard the words "unconditional surrender," since WW II from any President? Perhaps Truman should have demanded the same from North Korea and it would not be the threat that it is today.

Monday, January 9, 2017 at 10:28pm EST

I feel sorry for Mexico having to pay later for building the Great Wall of Trump. I don't like Congress appropriating big money for it to be erected. Trump should call for volunteers. There are countless contractors and masons, who are retired or semi-retired, who would be glad to be a part. Why not at least give it a try? It could become the patriotic thing to do. Muslims can stay at home. Mexicans, who are here illegally, could be put on fast road to citizenship for volunteering their labor for a year.

Tuesday, January 10, 2017 at 9:27pm EST

Obama in his Farewell Address is rattling on about race. The electorate determined it was tired of hearing racial rhetoric over and over. There will be a new trumpet in the White House.

Tuesday, January 10, 2017 at 9:39pm EST

Obama talks about reducing money in politics. Hillary far outspent Trump in the election.

Tuesday, January 10, 2017 at 9:55pm EST

It's over! That is the first Obama speech I have ever watched and listened to. Step up, Mr. Trump.

Wednesday, January 11, 2017 at 8:56pm EST

I have been waiting for this all of my life. The libs still don't know what hit them. Even Republicans can't figure Trump out. It's is going to be fun to watch the next 8 years! Spiro Agnew would be so proud of Trump.

Thursday, January 12, 2017 at 11:02pm EST

Trump's orders to his son, Barron, *"Remember, no alcohol, no drugs, no cigarettes, no tattoos."* He gave this advice to all of his children. Evidently, he has pulled it off. Good for him and good for them.

Friday, January 13, 2017 at 12:03am EST

The Trump's way to success is, *"know your product, love what you do and never give up."* His advice is applicable to the business world but it also applies to spreading the gospel.

Saturday, January 14, 2017 at 5:07pm EST
Kellyanne Conway broke the glass ceiling that Hillary merely butted her arrogant head against. Kellyanne is now arguably the most influential woman on the world stage. Plus, she is prettier, more articulate and possesses more poise than Hillary or Merkel. She is a true feminist in that she was able to maintain her femininity, which the other afore mentioned females lost somewhere along the way--if they ever had it. Of course, Ms. Conway could not have done it without the Donald to lead.

Wednesday, January 18, 2017 at 8:55am EST
At Florida State University yesterday a student was reading, *"The Art of the Deal,"* by Donald J. Trump. I asked the boy what he thought of the book. He answered, *"He seems larger than life."*

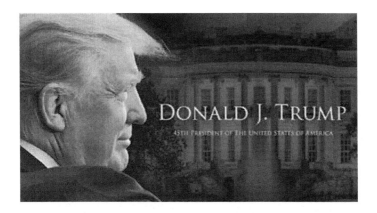

Chapter 4

The Inauguration

"What truly matters is not which party controls our government, but whether our government is controlled by the people. January 20th, 2017 will be remembered as the day the people became the rulers of this nation again. The forgotten men and women of our country will be forgotten no longer. Everyone is listening to you now. You came by the tens of millions to become part of a historic movement, the likes of which the world has never seen before. At the center of this movement is a crucial conviction that a nation exists to serve its citizens," President Donald Trump, Inaugural Address, 2017.

I DID IT MY WAY

Wednesday, January 18, 2017 at 10:16am EST

I don't care a wit that the Democrat Congressmen are boycotting the Inaugural. Makes room for those who appreciate the historical changing of the guard. Or should I say reestablishment of the guard? My heart is with Mr. Trump and Mr. Pence in Washington D.C. as Mikhail, Cindy and I preach to students at FSU. Yesterday, tracts were being passed out on campus encouraging a walkout of classes on Inauguration Day.

Wednesday, January 18, 2017 at 7:40pm EST

For those who like Trump: What is your Trump story? When and how did you become convinced to be a Trump supporter?

Thursday, January 19, 2017 at 9:56am EST

Being a compassionate man, I am going to try to empathize with the Democrats. I will have to admit that if Hillary had won I would not be paying any attention to her Inauguration. I could not bear hearing about her breaking the glass ceiling, the historical significance of the first woman president, blah, blah, blah. I could not stand to hear the speculation about what she would be wearing; nor could I stomach seeing the broad in another pant suit.

I did not watch either Obama Inauguration. I did not care that he was the first black president, yada, yada, yada. I had his number before he even announced that he was seeking the Democrat nomination.

I suppose the Democrats can't stand to hear about making America Great Again. Certainly, they don't want to hear about America First. Their vision is not for America; they are internationalists; I guess the term these days is globalists.

Thursday, January 19, 2017
Florida State University
I exposed the lie that Jesus was some kind of socialist. Of course, I had to brag on the Donald some of the time. All in all, it was a productive day. I left things in the hands of Mikhail to go back to the room to see Trump's Make America Great Again rally. Mikhail got back in time to see some of the entertainment and to hear Trump's talk to his tens of thousands of supporters. Speculation is that it was the greatest crowd ever gathered on the Mall.

Thursday, January 19, 2017 at 4:44pm EST
Sam Moore led an all-black choir in *America the Beautiful*. Sang with soul comparable to Ray Charles, with the wonderful Trump family present on the steps of the Lincoln Memorial. Trump said during his campaign that after four years he will get 95 % of the "black vote." It won't surprise me a bit.

Thursday, January 19, 2017 at 4:48pm EST
Fox is cutting away from the Trump rally to interview a Senator. Who wants to hear him? CNN stayed focused on the rally.

Thursday, January 19, 2017 at 5:07pm EST
John Voight gave God's perspective on Trump, wonderful introduction.

Thursday, January 19, 2017 at 5:27pm EST
Trump's musical taste is the pits!

Thursday, January 19, 2017 at 6:28pm EST
Charles Krauthammer said Trump's message fell short. Krauthammer has been wrong from the beginning about Trump and he continues to be. Will this man ever learn to shut up?

Thursday, January 19, 2017 at 9:12pm EST
In a speech tonight Trump is acknowledging the help of Phyllis Schlafly in his campaign. She "went through hell in helping me." Her opposition came mainly from other Conservatives. Trump went to her funeral. I appreciate Trump acknowledging her.

Thursday, January 19, 2017 at 9:14pm EST
"There is no den in which my Kellyanne won't go into to defend me. She will go on networks where the men won't go," said Donald J. Trump.

Thursday, January 19, 2017 at 11:15pm EST
I am so impressed with the way Trump's children honor him and the whole family works together with him in leadership to promote the cause or the movement to Make America Great Again. This is the way God intended families to work. Notice how Trump makes every effort to give credit to his great parents for his success.

Thursday, January 19, 2017 at 11:39pm EST
I get Trump's usage of the Rolling Stone's, *"You Can't Always Get What You Want."* But I can't figure out why he wanted to walk the steps of Lincoln's Memorial with Melania to the song, *"A Heart of Stone."* Maybe he just likes the beat? Do any FB friends have an explanation?

Friday, January 20, 2017 at 9:46am EST
Mrs. Trump's outfit is modest and appropriate. In my day, women always wore gloves for formal occasions. Good for her; she will make a great First Lady.

Friday, January 20, 2017 at 11:40am EST
Cardinal Dolan gave good prayer on the need for wisdom. Wisdom is the principle thing said Solomon.

Friday, January 20, 2017 at 11:43am EST
Way to go, Paula White, strong Trinitarian prayer in the name of Jesus. I knew she would do well.

Friday, January 20, 2017 at 11:49am EST
Shut up Schumer! Who let him up there?

Friday, January 20, 2017 at 11:55am EST
VP Pence, he was the perfect choice.

Friday, January 20, 2017 at 11:57am EST
The Mormons have promoted much goodwill through their choir.

Friday, January 20, 2017 at 12:02pm EST
It is done; it is just beginning!

Friday, January 20, 2017 at 12:11pm EST
He is real! He is promoting his campaign promises. I knew he was sincere.

Friday, January 20, 2017 at 12:13pm EST
America is back!

Friday, January 20, 2017 at 12:15pm EST
We will be protected by God, says our President!

Friday, January 20, 2017 at 12:15pm EST
This is his greatest speech ever!

Waited a Lifetime

Friday, January 20, 2017 at 12:19pm EST
I have been waiting to hear this all my life. I am glad that I have lived to hear it. Now I look forward to seeing it. And doing it!

Friday, January 20, 2017 at 12:21pm EST
Good job, Rabbi!

Friday, January 20, 2017 at 12:24pm EST
Quick thinking, Franklin Graham, about the significance of the rain falling on President Trump!

Friday, January 20, 2017 at 12:26pm EST
God is back in America. This is by far the most Christian Inaugural in my lifetime.

Friday, January 20, 2017
Florida State University
We watched the Inauguration in our motel room. After Trump's address, Mikhail walked over to campus to start the meeting. I arrived about 1:45 PM. A number of students cheered when they saw me coming. After several days on campus, especially the ones we preach on annually, we have our fans.

"There should not be fear," Trump said in his Inaugural address. *"We are protected and we will always be protected. We will be protected by the great men and women of our military and law enforcement, and, most important, we will be protected by God."*

Friday, January 20, 2017 at 3:13pm EST
Twice I have seen Fox cut away from a prayer for chit chat. CNN cameras remained on the one praying. The prayers may be the most important part of the Inaugural events. Some of these pundits are so self-centered; they consider their own words more important than God's.

Friday, January 20, 2017 at 6:32pm EST
I enjoy marching bands with sharp uniforms. It seems bands, especially high school bands, are not as prominent as they used to be. Unfortunately, the bands' uniforms have become too casual, not so in the Inaugural parade. Trump likes pomp and circumstance, maybe he will usher in a revival of marching bands.

Friday, January 20, 2017 at 6:35pm EST
Trump has been standing throughout this long parade. The man never seems to tire. He has had a long, active and what would be for any other man a stressful time.

Now he has the Inaugural Balls to attend. And he is still going strong.

Friday, January 20, 2017 at 8:25pm EST
Wearing the pant suit until the bitter end.

Friday, January 20, 2017 at 8:29pm EST
I must confess I have grown fond of the Carters over the years. Also, since Trump is expressing a positive attitude towards Obama and Michele, my heart may be softening just a little bit towards them, especially now that they are out of power. *(short-lived)*

Friday, January 20, 2017 at 9:05pm EST
For those who may have missed it, here is the invocation delivered by Paula White, pastor of the New Destiny Christian Center:

> *We come to you, heavenly Father, in the name of Jesus with grateful hearts, thanking you for this great country that you have decreed to your people. We acknowledge we are a blessed nation with a rich history of faith and fortitude, with a future that is filled with promise and purpose.*
>
> *We recognize that every good and every perfect gift comes from you and the United States of America is your gift, for which we proclaim our gratitude.*
>
> *As a nation, we now pray for our president, Donald John Trump, vice president, Michael Richard Pence, and their families. We ask that you would bestow upon our president the wisdom necessary to lead this great nation, the grace to*

unify us, and the strength to stand for what is honorable and right in your sight.

In Proverbs 21:1, you instruct us that our leader's heart is in your hands. Gracious God, reveal unto our president the ability to know your will, the confidence to lead us in justice and righteousness, and the compassion to yield to our better angels.

While we know there are many challenges before us, in every generation you have provided the strength and power to become that blessed nation. Guide us in discernment, Lord, and give us that strength to persevere and thrive.

Now bind and heal our wounds and divisions, and join our nation to your purpose. Thy kingdom come, thy will be done, the psalmists declared.

Let your favor be upon this one nation under God. Let these United States of America be that beacon of hope to all people and nations under your dominion, a true hope for humankind.

Glory to the Father, the Son, and the Holy Spirit. We pray this in the name of Jesus Christ. Amen.

Friday, January 20 at 11:30 pm EST

When the Trumps arrived at the Inaugural Ball, the President said, *"We did it. We began this journey and they said ... we didn't have a chance but we knew we were going to win and we won."*

The pundits predicted that Hillary would waltz to the Presidency. But to her shock, she was not even asked to the big dance.

Instead at the Inaugural Ball, the Trumps danced to Frank Sinatra's greatest hit, *"My Way."* And the

President mouthed some of the words, while he held Melania's hand near his heart.

Indeed, he did it his way, when the establishment of the Republican Party, the Democrats, and the pundits repeatedly said to the very end, *"He can't do it this way!"*

**"And more, much more than this
I did it my way."**

"He can't accuse Mexicans of being murderers, rapists, drug dealers and get the nomination. Trump will implode with his own words. He doesn't have a ground game. He doesn't have the organization. He's not a conservative. He is not mentally sound. He is not Presidential. He throws temper tantrums on Twitter."

**"I did what I had to do
And saw it through without exception"**

They predicted, *"His candidacy went from boom to bust when he criticized McCain for being captured during the Vietnam War. He can't question and oppose Bush's war in Iraq and expect to be the party's standard bearer. He can't make fun of a handicapped man; it will finish him."*

**"I planned each charted course
Each careful step along the byway
Oh, and more, much more than this
I did it my way."**

Each week it was something new during the Primaries, then in the General Election, that was bound to bring about the end of his run but he kept gaining in the opinion polls and winning primaries.

They said, *"What worked in the Primaries will never work in the General Election."* When he received the nomination, the pundits were all saying he had to pivot, but he never did.

"He can't attack a five-star family and expect to be president. He cannot say the crude things he has said about women and win."

"He can't build the wall! He can't make Mexico pay for it! He can't prevent Muslims from entering the country. He can't drain the swamp. There is no way for him to get the necessary electoral votes; he has no path to the presidency. The reality is that leaders in the Republican Party know he can't win."

Tonight, his opponents were all still in shock, months after his election when the lord of the Ball danced with his wife.

> *"For what is a man, what has he got*
> *If not himself, then he has not*
> *To say the things he truly feels*
> *And not the words he would reveal*
> *The record shows I took the blows*
> *And did it my way."*

He proved all his enemies wrong in every instance. He did it; he did it his way! He became lord of the biggest dance in the Free World.

> *"For I am the lord of the dance, said he*
> *And I'll lead you all wherever you may be*
> *And I'll lead you all in the dance, said he."*

Saturday, January 21, 2017 at 10:34am EST

The Christian service was yesterday morning led by Pastor Jeffries. Unfortunately, there will be other expressions of religion at the National Cathedral service, including Islam. Father Sirico said, *"This service is a civic expression of religion."*

The service opened with a Christian hymn, *Faith of our Fathers.*

Saturday, January 21, 2017 at 3:20pm EST

Paula White says Donald Trump is saved.

Saturday, January 21, 2017 at 9:17pm EST

"His message to America: Remember those things I said in the campaign? I meant them. I meant it all," Peggy Noonan.

To answer your question at the end of your well written article, yes, we Trump supporters do understand the difficulties ahead. We believe we can do it with the leadership of the President, Donald J. Trump.

Saturday, January 21, 2017 at 10:22pm EST

The Democrats have for a long time accused Republicans of a war on women. Sounds like the protesting feminists in Washington D.C. today want to fight back.

What if Republican men and leftist women actually took up arms between one another? Who would win? Maybe the feminists could get the wussy Democrat men to fight with them, but I don't think they would be much help.

The Democrats have been promoting a phony war between blacks and whites for decades, which has never come to pass. The riotous blacks will not get away with it anymore with Jeff Sessions and Donald J. Trump in place.

Democrats are all about promoting warfare between workers and management, blacks and whites and men and women. What else would we expect from Marxists? Trump has been winning over some key blacks with true leadership skills and not simply rabble rousers like Sharpton and his gang. Plus, real women love Donald J. Trump.

Sunday, January 22, 2017 at 5:59pm EST

A Navajo Indian with a painted face chanted the Invocation at the Inaugural prayer service at the National Cathedral. It is appropriate that the meeting started with the Indian to show us savagery and to reveal what our country would be like had not Christians introduced civilization to the New World.

Actually, the heathen's invocation was appropriate to the occasion: *"With beauty before me I walk. With beauty behind me I walk. With beauty above me I walk. With beauty around me I walk. It has become beauty again. It has become beauty again. It has become beauty again. It has become beauty again."*

America the Beautiful had been restored with President Trump, who knows and loves our heritage, who intends to make America Great Again. He will put our beloved nation back in her place as the Shining City upon the Hill.

Sunday, January 22, 2017 at 6:30pm EST

Not only did God speak through the Indian at the National Inaugural Prayer Service, but he also spoke through the Rabbi: The First Reading was 1 Kings 3:5–12, Rabbi Fred Raskind, Temple Bet Yam, St. Augustine, Florida. Solomon prayed at Gibeon: *"Your servant finds himself in the midst of the people You have chosen, a people too numerous to be numbered or counted. Grant, then, Your servant an understanding mind to judge Your people, to distinguish between good and bad; for who can judge this vast people of Yours?" The Lord was pleased that Solomon had asked for this. And God said to him, "Because you asked for this—you did not ask for long life, you did not ask for riches, you did not ask for the life of your enemies, but you asked for discernment in dispensing justice—I now do as you have spoken. I grant you a wise and discerning mind; there has never been anyone like you before, nor will anyone like you arise again."*

Although the text applies to Solomon, as a former instructor in history at the University of Wisconsin, Lacrosse, I would have to say there has never been a man like Trump, who has ascended to the presidency--nor is it likely there will ever be another like him. The wisdom that God has granted to Trump is simple common sense, which is available to us all.

Regrettably, college educated people have been brainwashed cleanly from what they intuitively know as right and wrong. It took the populous, the common folks, who had the wisdom to recognize a leader and to exalt such a man to the highest office of our land.

Chapter 5

First 100 Days

I Will Not Let You Down
—President Trump.

Roll On Trump Train!

Sunday, January 22, 2017 at 11:09pm EST

I am excited about Trump's first work day in the Oval Office. What executive orders of Obama will he reverse? Had Hillary won, it would be the same old, same old, zzzzzzzzzzzzzzzz. She put me to sleep, so did Obama. Common folks everywhere are waking up from a long dark night that has spanned both Democrat and Republican administrations. President Trump may bring about a political awakening throughout the world.

Monday, January 23, 2017 at 10:27pm EST

Our right-handed president signed three executive actions today. It is good to have a righty in the White House again after 28 years of left-handed presidents, except for eight years of G.W. I say this as a left-hander myself, with one exception; I always batted right, which was a big mistake, since the batter on the left side of the plate has one less step to first base.

BRO JED'S REVIEW OF
THE ART OF THE DEAL
Monday, January 23, 2017

During the campaign, I read much of Donald Trump's, *"The Art of the Deal."* I considered it an inspiration and it gave me a better understanding of the character of the man and his preparation to be president.

The book spent one year on the NY Times best-seller list from the date of its publication in 1987. Back then, it seemed Trump's face was featured in the window of every bookstore. Nevertheless, the book did not interest me until last year as I became curious about Trump.

In the late 70's and early 80's I began a serious study of economics, especially the Austrian school. I became well-versed in free-market economics through independent study and meditation. I frequently wrote on the subject.

Over the decades, I have debated capitalism vs. socialism in both informal and formal debates with both students and professors, and in recent years online. For all those decades I was more interested in defending free markets intellectually, than I was in making money or making deals.

Both the economic study and the commercial action have their place. Jesus said at 12 years old, *"Know you not that I must be about my father's business."* Paul admonishes, *"Be not slothful in business."*

Winning souls has been and remains my primary business. To do that, I need health and wealth, which is a reason for me be supportive of faith teachers on these subjects.

Men who have worked hard or are laboring hard to create wealth are the economic engine of my ministry. The Trump presidency will favor business over big government; business is the catalyst to make America great again; we preachers are the agents to make the church great again.

I admire Trump for the economic empire he has built. Socialists are basically covetous; they resent anyone who has more than they do. They are out to redistribute existing wealth instead of making wealth. They are losers; Trump is a winner, now, not only in the business realm but also the political world. The art of knowing how to make a deal will no doubt help him greatly as he negotiates with Congress, hostile governments and a corrupt media.

Wednesday, January 25, 2017 at 4:53am EST

As I scan my newsfeed, I have noticed a trend of false news reports concerning the President's actions or policies that are based on wishful thinking on the part of Christians and conservatives, and fear on the part of the heathens and liberals.

Under Obama there were false news reports based on fear from the right, such as Obama preparing to establish martial law. The difference is that under Obama, there was no basis for wishful thinking from the right. I guess it is fun to wish sometimes, but let's not get carried away, folks.

Wednesday, January 25, 2017 at 11:03am EST

I did not know there were female secret service agents, figures though. I can understand why Mr. Trump keeps his own security detail. There were reports of the SS partying and carousing during the Obama years. I would not trust them. Does not speak well of this agency.

Alas, it appears that virtually all government agencies are not what they once were. When I was young, the FBI was held in high esteem. J. Edgar Hoover protected the reputation of his agency. The Post Office was also highly respected, but it has never been the same since the postal strike.

Wednesday, January 25, 2017 at 9:28pm EST
The rule of law is restored and the wall is going to be built. Thank you, President Trump! You, sir, are a great American.

Friday, January 27, 2017 at 4:27am EST
I can't remember anything that Trump has done or said since he threw his hat in the ring, that I have not enjoyed. And it gets better every day! I suppose at some point he will do something I don't like, but so far it has been a fast and exciting ride on the Trump train.

Friday, January 27, 2017 at 11:36am EST
The Trumpster is going to get the dirty rats!

Monday, January 30, 2017 at 6:09am EST
President Trump has a portrait of President Andrew Jackson hanging in the Oval Office. "Old Hickory" helped Make America Great; Trump will Make America Great Again.

"Kick'em the Hell Outta Here"

Monday, January 30, 2017 at 9:37am EST
All this phony concern about some foreigners being detained as a result of the President's order, what about the American travelers, who may have been inconvenienced in in their travels by the protestors? There must have been significant delays by passengers and those picking up friends and family at the airports.

Monday, January 30, 2017 at 10:37am EST

After I graduated college in the summer of 1965, I toured Europe. When in Berlin, I got a visa to enter East Berlin for a day. Somehow my visa was either lost or stolen. Upon my return to the Berlin Wall, I was detained and interrogated for several hours by various communist agents before being allowed to leave the East.

About a year later, I got a call from the U.S. State Dept. informing me that they received a report that I had been in East Berlin helping people escape to the West. I was warned not to return to East Berlin without first informing the State Department. Today, this is one of the most memorable incidents of my European tour.

Three decades ago, I decided to preach in England. I made the mistake of telling immigration officials that I had come to England to preach the gospel. I was detained for a few hours before being allowed to enter the country. Since then, when going to a foreign country, I simply say, "I am a tourist."

Evidently, immigration officials were concerned about people from the Hare Krishna cult entering their country. Foreigners do not have a natural right to enter another country. Nations do have a basic right to protect their borders. I do not resent the East Germans or England for detaining me for a time. To them, I was a suspicious character. I noticed that one detained man informed the media that he liked Trump.

The airport protestors may have been more upset about the problems of entry than most of the foreigners, who were actually detained or sent back. Foreigners just ought to be thankful that they are allowed in America.

BTW, I know that it is politically incorrect to call people "foreigners" instead of "internationals." Thank

God we can be politically incorrect again, thanks to Donald J. Trump.

Monday, January 30, 2017 at 7:15pm EST

Can President Donald J. Trump not only Make America Great Again but Western Civilization, which used to be called Christendom, as well? He is shaking up the Western World.

Monday, January 30, 2017 at 11:04pm EST

Oh boy, Trump has fired that woman! (Sally Yates, Acting Attorney General.)

Tuesday, January 31, 2017 at 12:57am EST

What is this with Schumer crying? As I watched the Inaugural, the commentators wondered if Trump would cry. Some suggested he ought to cry to show a softer side. Can't think of the name of the former Republican Speaker who would cry at the drop of a hat. What is all this crying about? Is it the influence of women entering the political and media world, or what? Yes, I know Jesus wept but that was over the lost condition of the Jews in Jerusalem.

Tuesday, January 31, 2017 at 10:32am EST

My friend, Rocket Kirchner from Columbia, MO, texted me, "Trump is Ty Cobb." I like the comparison. I am inspired by men who reach legendary status. Aren't we all? The legends interest me more than the actual facts. Fact and fiction are often difficult to separate anyway.

Tuesday, January 31, 2017 at 10:37am EST

I watched Trump's meeting with the CEOs of big pharmacy. The president promised to eliminate 75 to 80% of the government regulations on the industry.

GOD IS A WALLBUILDER
Wednesday, February 1, 2017
Stephen F. Austin University

At around 5 PM I gave the students a parting shot, *"Thank you for choosing Donald J. Trump for president. The good people of Texas favored him overwhelmingly. The country owes a debt to you Trump supporters."*

The students were outraged, assuring me that they did not vote for Trump.

I shot again, *"Trump's going to build many miles of wall right here at your southern border. It is going to be a great and beautiful wall."*

Then somebody read Lev. 19:34, *"The stranger who resides with you shall be to you as the native among you, and you shall love him as yourself, for you were aliens in the land of Egypt; I am the LORD your God."*

"Immigrants that come here legally we should treat as we would ourselves. For the illegals, we need a wall to keep them out," I responded.

I continued, *"God likes walls; he has a wall around his kingdom. Jesus said,*

> *'Enter ye in at the strait gate: for wide is the gate, and broad is the way, that leadeth to destruction, and many there be which go in thereat: Because strait is the gate, and narrow is the way, which leadeth unto life, and few there be that find it.'—Matt 7:13-14.*

God only establishes a loving relationship with those who repent and obey the gospel. Everyone else is kept outside the wall.

Where there is a gate, there must be a wall. God implements extreme vetting as to whom he allows through the narrow gate into Kingdom of Heaven.

The Great Wall of Trump will have many gates allowing legal immigrants but keeping out the illegals."

Thursday, February 2, 2017 at 5:02pm EST
I told the vixen at Sam Houston State wearing the "F**k Trump" hat that she could not have sex with Trump as much as she may want to.

Thursday, February 2, 2017 at 9:37pm EST
Trump is John Wayne; Trump is True Grit.
I wore my Trump socks to campus today.

Saturday, February 4, 2017 at 10:57am EST
Trump is a man uniquely prepared for the office. *"And who knoweth whether thou art come to the kingdom for such a time as this?"*--Esther 4:14.

Missionary Mitch Metzger, *"I am so excited to be living, and experiencing, the multiple applications, and leadership styles of Trump. I think he is doing a great job. His whole life, he has been preparing for this. His gifts, business experiences, personality profile, life experiences, and God's favor, are all in convergence."*

Herman Cain's article is the most insightful piece that I have read on our President's extraordinary strategy:

> *"One of the biggest mistakes of the political establishment - one they show no sign of grasping - is that when they*

constantly complain about how Trump is violating all the norms of politics, the presidency and international relations, they totally miss that this is exactly what the people who voted for him wanted him to do. And they totally miss that he is doing it intentionally and with purpose.

Establishment voices think Trump is an out-of-control bumpkin who has no idea what the proper way is to operate on the world stage. They think he's going around upsetting people because of his insatiable ego, or because of his anger, or because of some secret and nefarious agenda he has. If that's what you think, you'll constantly miss the meaning of Trump's actions, which is clear as day from his patterns if you're willing to see it.

Trump knows perfectly well that his actions are disrupting the global status quo, and upsetting people who don't want to have to get used to a different way of dealing with the United States. That's what he's trying to do. Why? Because other nations have no incentive to reconsider the status quo unless they're afraid an American acting unilaterally will impose a different and much more unsettling new status quo. Trump needs to get both allies and adversaries feeling like they'd better get in front of him and work something out, and quickly.

And in case you hadn't noticed, just as the news media consistently takes Trump's bait, foreign leaders are doing the exact same thing.

So the "global anxiety" is having the intended effect. Allies are rushing for face time with Trump because they know it's a new day, and they're going to have to deal with him. When a new player arrives on the scene and he doesn't follow the established rules, traditions or norms - and doesn't appear to feel bound by the boundaries that limited the maneuvers of his predecessors - what do you do? You could denounce him. You could vow never to work with him. But he's got a bigger gun than you do, and you need his help..."

Saturday, February 4, 2017 at 10:51pm EST

I am not a football fan but I am rooting for Brady since he is the old guy. If he wins, he will be the oldest quarterback (39) to win the Super Bowl. I always rooted for the old guys, even when I was young. Plus, Brady is friends with the President. Therefore, libs don't like him. If libs don't like him, there must be a lot to like about Brady.

Sunday, February 5, 2017 at 8:40am EST

I am hereby naming and claiming President Donald J. Trump as a brother in Christ.

Sunday, February 5, 2017 at 5:46pm EST

The Twilight Zone ran on TV from 1959-64. Shortly afterwards, America began to darken into the Twilight Zone, which was in full swing by the "Summer of Love" in 1967 at the Haight Asbury in San Francisco.

Hopefully, after eight years of the blackness of darkness during the Obama years, we are experiencing a new dawning with the Era of Trump--a return to common sense. The devil is tenaciously trying to hold on in the light of his recent major loss.

Sunday, February 5, 2017 at 11:11pm EST

Oliver Cromwell, Lord Protectorate of England, Scotland and Ireland, 1599-1658, said, *"Not only strike while the iron is hot, but make it hot by striking."*

Reminds me of the first two weeks of Brother Donald J. Trump's presidency. So far Trump hasn't struck so hard as Cromwell. I mean both Hillary and Obama still have their heads, unlike Charles I.

Monday, February 6, 2017 at 10:32pm EST

Why do Brit politicians object to a Trump visit? Could it be that they are afraid that he will be popularly received by the people?

Monday, February 6, 2017
Texas A&M

Cindy drew a large crowd at noon. As she was speaking, several students greeted me warmly on the sidelines. One compared our approach to Donald Trump's, who is always stirring up the fire.

Draining the Swamp

Tuesday, February 7, 2017 at 1:22pm EST
The Trump train keeps rolling over everyone who gets in its way. Today it was the Teachers' Union and educational establishment. Brother Pence cast a tie breaking historical vote confirming the home schooling mom, Betsy Ross (I mean Devos), as Education Secretary. Praise the Lord!

Pocahontas (Warren) is on the warpath; her feminist frenzied face represents the Democratic Party and she has become the voice of liberalism. Whoop! Whoop! Whoop! She is shriller than Hillary and will be scalped by Trump. Americans want their public women to look like Melania and Ivanka and to talk like Kellyanne.

Tuesday, February 14, 2017 at 11:37am EST
Vigo County is my home; Cindy and I are still Trumped Up! (*For more than a hundred years, Vigo County, Indiana has consistently voted for the winning president.*)

Tuesday, February 14, 2017 at 10:33pm EST
We all know that when Trump is punched, he counterpunches. The left knocked General Flynn out of the ring. Now, who should Trump take a swing against? Surely he will not take this sitting down. The enemy is within.

Goodness TRUMPS Evil

Tuesday, February 14, 2017 at 10:47pm EST
I hope President Trump's spiritual advisors are directing him towards reading the Psalms of David. His enemies are much like David's. I call Christians to pray the imprecatory Psalms against The President's enemies, which remain in high places. I am daily putting on the whole armor of God. I have the President's back. How about you, fellow Christian? The battle has begun. We must prevail. Our beloved country is at stake. Not all of Trump's enemies are Democrats. Trump has his enemies within the party. You know who they are.

Friday, February 17, 2017 at 9:52am EST
One of my favorite points of Trump's press conference was when he said he was not going to tell the media what he was going to do about North Korea and Iran and other hostile powers, because that would be signaling and thus preparing our enemies. The press thinks they have a right to know; then as soon as they are told, they began criticizing. They think they ought to have an input in forming foreign policy. It's a new day in America.

Saturday, February 18, 2017 at 12:30am EST
Donald J. Trump is the man whose presence always fills the room. The other Republican candidates were like the seven dwarfs compared to Snow White. Snow White's vindictive step mother, the Wicked Queen, is obsessed, *"Mirror, mirror on the wall, who is the fairest of them all?"* She tries to kill the fairest Snow White.
In the resolution of the original fairy tale, the good Prince and Snow White invite the Queen to their

wedding, where she is forced to put on red-hot shoes and dance until she drops dead. Crooked Hillary is the narcissistic and prideful would-be Queen, who loses to the humble Prince Trump. In the end, goodness Trumps evil. All presidents since Reagan, especially Obama, dwarf in comparison to the Donald.

Saturday, February 18, 2017 at 10:24pm EST
Sister Melania Trump invokes the Lord's Prayer to open campaign rally for 2020. I never heard a First Lady or a President say this: *"Thy kingdom come, Thy will be done, in earth as it is in heaven..."*

God's servants, the Trumps, will labor to see that God's will is done in the world. There has been speculation concerning the President's faith, not so much on the faith of his wife. Now we know. After the First Lady prayed and spoke softly for a few minutes, the Lion roared for an hour speaking of what we have already done and what he will yet do to Make America Great Again.

Let us pray that our President will be diligent to bear the sword, *for the he is the minister of God, a revenger to execute God's wrath upon evildoers* (Romans 13:4).

Mad Dog Mattis is working on the plan right now to fulfil another Trump campaign promise to defeat ISIS. Folks, we are in good hands.

Friday, February 24, 2017 at 11:00pm EST
"This is the U.S of America I'm representing; I'm not representing the globe. I'm representing your country," Trump tells the Conservative Political Action Conference on Friday.

Friday, February 24, 2017 at 11:05pm EST

Was "Deep Throat" fake news? Did the Washington Post make this person up? I know many years after the scandal, we were told who this unidentified source was supposed to be. But how do we know we were finally actually told the truth? If Nixon can see and hear Trump, he must be cheering him on.

Saturday, February 25, 2017 at 12:29am EST

I would like to see President Trump not make any visits to foreign nations. Let the foreign leaders come to him. Presidents spend far too much time abroad. Their trips are very expensive. Trump's pledged to put America first. T.R. was the first president to go abroad; he visited the Panama Canal in 1906.

Our Lionhearted President

Sunday, February 26, 2017 at 11:37pm EST

Hereby I do dub thee, President Trump the Lionheart.

Monday, February 27 at 8:17 pm EST

What makes the lion *"the King of the Jungle?"* Is it his strength? Is it his fierceness and his boldness? Is it his regal bearing and magnificent presence?

There are animals that are bigger and stronger and have more stamina than the lion, there are animals that are faster, there are beasts that are even better hunters, but what makes the lion arguably the most fearsome animal to walk the grasslands is his ferocious roar, his voice is reputation.

President Trump the Lionheart has become *"the King of the Jungle,"* because his fierce roar gives voice to harsh realities that have captivated America and the world. Although he is one of the most successful and richest men of our time, he speaks the common sense of the common man, who is his main constituency.

Trump, like a lion, also has strength, boldness and a presidential bearing. Trump's stamina is more legendary than a lion. A lion sleeps up to 20 hours a day; whereas Trump works 20 hours a day and sleeps only four hours.

Tuesday, February 28 at 10:43am
The distinctive physical feature of the male lion is his mane. They say that the mane attracts the lionesses and provides protection for his neck from other animals with which he may fight. Lion coloration varies from light buff to yellowish or even reddish. Trump's craggy eyebrows and his mane which varies from blond to orange, along with his large stature set him apart and give him a lion-like look.

Tuesday, February 28 at 9:20pm EST
There are two things Trump said that I did not like. Does anyone have an idea of what they were?

He said we should work with our Muslim friends to destroy ISIS. We should be very cautious if we are going to do this. I don't trust any of them. If we are going to defeat ISIS, help from Muslims ought to be at a minimum.

I do not think there should be any guarantees that people with pre-existing conditions should be insured.

Tuesday, February 28 at 9:22 pm EST
Melania Trump knows how to carry herself. She has poise unlike any First Lady of my lifetime. It may be a

result of her modeling training or some ladies just naturally seem to have it. Melania certainly had a look on her face that she was proud of her husband during his address.

Tuesday, February 28 at 10:03pm EST·
My favorite quote from Trump's speech before Congress: *"My job is not to represent the world. My job is to represent the United States of America."*

LION AND HYENA ETERNAL ENEMIES
Wednesday, March 1, 2017
The lion and the hyena are eternal enemies. Both animals are scavengers and compete for prey. Lions are considered noble, dignified and courageous, while hyenas are regarded as lowly, demonic and cowardly. Biblically, Christ is known as *"The Lion of the Tribe of Judah."*

No one would ever consider hyenas comparable to Jesus. Jesus spoke of false prophets and teachers as wolves in sheep's clothing. Hyenas are wolf-like in appearance, except hyenas are sloped backed with high forelegs and low hind legs with short thick necks. They are ugly beasts, whereas wolves at least have a certain outward attraction. Lions are regal, especially the male with his mane, which is his crown.

While lions roar to scare their enemies, hyenas produce heinous noises--whoops, grunts, groans, lows, giggles, yells, growls, and whines, when they are fighting for prey. They are especially known for their screeching laugh but it is not a laugh of joy. We have heard of humans laughing hysterically like a hyena.

Hyenas are commonly viewed as frightening and worthy of contempt, and are associated with witchcraft, because their body parts have been used as ingredients in witches' brews. Some people think hyenas are physical incarnations of demons, which rob graves, and steal livestock and children. Hyenas are often considered symbols of treachery and stupidity.

The lion-like President Trump's main competitor is the Democratic Party. Democrats are contemptuous like the hyenas. Trump and the Democrats are competing for voters, enough of whom answered his roar to Make America Great Again and to make him the leader of the pride of lions, which is the Republican Party.

The Democrats put their faith in a witch to attempt to poison the minds of Americans against our lion leader. The witch could laugh hysterically and when she attempted to roar it sounded more like whining and yelling.

Democrats are traitors towards the American heritage of limited government, individual responsibility and private property. Thankfully, the electorate rose up and voted them out of office.

Democrats are stupid in that they usually overreach when they are in authority. But the lion has awakened with a thunderous roar and is chasing away the Democrats from leadership in the legislative and executive branches of government. Next the liberals will be driven from the judicial branch. The lion will remain victorious as, *"the King of the Jungle."*

Wednesday, March 1 at 9:03pm EST
Trump the Lionheart is surrounded by Schumer, Pelosi, Obama, and the hyenas in the media. Hillary has already been killed.

Sunday, March 5 at 6:28am EST·
Micah Armstrong has been in the forefront in his bold and early support of Trump.

Bro. Micah posted: *"Given President Trump's history of accuracy and vindication I am tempted to ask as was of King Saul, 'Is President Trump also among the prophets?'"*

Monday, March 6 at 11:55pm EST
Donald J. Trump is a humble man. Most people do not perceive that character quality in him, but the common man and business man see it and they respect Trump for it.

Trump does not have a self-deprecating sense of humor like G.W. and even Reagan practiced at times. I never cared for undervaluing oneself, even in humor. No president in my memory has been attacked like Trump with the exception of Nixon. With the many who are belittling Trump, he need not belittle himself.

After Moses came down from Mt. Sinai, where he received the law, he had three thousand rebels put to death for their idolatry. The Scriptures then say of Moses that he was the meekest man on the face of the earth (Numbers 12:3).

Do you suppose the Pharaoh perceived Moses as humble? Did his own people see him as meek as they were constantly rebelling against him? But God saw the humility in Moses that others could not see because of their own pride.

God will use Mr. Trump mightily as he remains humble.

Tuesday, March 7 at 2:05 pm EST

The media and Democrats hate him; world leaders fear him. But the people that matter love Trump. He can speak directly to the people via Twitter. And despite the media hatred, they have to cover him since everyone wants to know what he has to say. The billionaire speaks the language of the common man. Long live the Trumpster!

Saturday, March 11 at 11:26 pm EST

Will the replacement of Obamacare be called Trumpcare? I hope not. It is not the role of government to provide health care for the populace. Hopefully, the replacement will at least wean Americans from the teats of the federal government.

Saturday, March 11 at 11:41 pm EST

Two things need to be done concerning the health care issue: 1. Eliminate the individual mandate, 2. Insurance companies should not be required to insure for pre-conditions.

We need to get back to basic principles, no one should be required to buy a product or service and no one should be force to sell a good or service.

Samson & Trump, Part 1
Sunday March 12, 2017

Samson, before he was conceived, was called of God to deliver Israel out of the hand of the Philistines. He was to be a Nazarite from his mother's womb and not to drink wine or strong drink.

Donald Trump does not drink, smoke or use drugs. And God has raised him up to deliver America out of the hand of the liberals, globalists, feminists and socialists.

When Samson was a young man, he was confronted by a lion, which roared against *him "and the Spirit of the LORD came mightily upon Samson and he rent the lion with his bare hands."*

In the Bible Jesus is portrayed as *"the Lion of the tribe of Judah"* and Satan is also pictured as a lion going about seeking to devour whom he will. After the lion killing incident, Samson's story emerges into a pattern that whenever he needed strength against the enemies of Israel, *"the Spirit of the LORD came mightily upon him."*

Samson's anger was often kindled to take vengeance against the Philistines. After one of his several one-man slaughters of the Philistines, they came down to Judah and demanded that Samson's people turn him over.

Three thousand men of Judah fearfully went to Samson and said, *"Knowest thou not that the Philistines are rulers over us? What is this that thou hast done unto us?"*

To think that Israel would conspire against their deliverer, their champion, their own son, Samson, is mind-boggling. But then, the Jews conspired against their own, brother, Jesus. Slaves, after a while, come to grips with their slavery and become fearful of a life of independence and freedom. They find a comfort in their serfdom. After God through Moses delivered his people out of 400 years of Egyptian bondage, they were always longing to return to Egypt and rebelling against Moses.

The establishment Republicans did what they could to discourage and defeat their champion, Trump, who is the only one who demonstrated that he had no fear of the Democrats and the media and was able to stand against them with impunity. Early on Trump demonstrated that he was more than any other Republican, able to gain support from the working class.

Republicans learned over many years to adapt to Democrat rule and doctrines, preferring accommodation over the rigors of economic freedom. Even after winning the nomination, then the Presidency, many still opposed their champion. Others have finally boarded the Trump train as it rolls down the track crushing those who stand in its way.

Samson answered the cowardly men of Judah, *"As they did unto me, so have I done unto them."*

Donald Trump is a man after Samson's own heart. When still only a businessman and entertainer, Trump tweeted on November 11, 2012, *"When someone attacks me, I always attack back...except 100x more. This has nothing to do with a tirade but rather, a way of life!"*

Trump's way of life triumphed over 16 Republicans, Hillary, the media, and even most voters to win the presidency of the United States. And he will continue to attack. He plays offense, while his V.P., Pence, plays defense! As the man, Trump, says, *"Believe me."*

The faint-hearted men of Judah said to Samson, *"We are come down to bind thee, that we may deliver thee into the hand of the Philistines."*

Samson allowed his countrymen to tie him with two new cords and turn him over to their enemies. However, when the Philistines prematurely shouted for victory, *"the Spirit of the LORD came mightily upon Samson, and his hands were loosed."*

Then, Samson took a jawbone of an ass, and put forth his hand, and took it, and slew a thousand Philistines.

The Democrats throughout the nominating process claimed that Trump would be the easiest one for Hillary to defeat. The conventional thinking from the Republicans was that any established Republican could beat Hillary handily with Trump being so supposedly unpopular, unconventional and controversial. But the Spirit of the LORD came mightily on Trump and he conquered Florida and the "Rust Belt," something which low energy Jeb would have never done, at least as far as Wisconsin, Michigan and Pennsylvania are concerned.

Samson rejoiced in song, *"With the jawbone of an ass, heaps upon heaps, with the jaw of an ass have I slain a thousand men."*

Trump, always the winner, danced and sang with his lovely wife at the Inaugural Ball, *"I Did It My Way,"* with the world watching in wonder and agreement. He surely did.

Samson escaped from what seemed impossible situations in his many fights with the Philistines and he did it singlehandedly.

Trump did it when all the pundits predicted time and time again that, finally, he had gone too far in his politically incorrect statements and actions. He would never recover, they predicted. But he just kept campaigning and working and continued to gather support underneath the radar of the opinion polls. The

Trump train kept on rolling, rolling, rolling. Nothing could stop it.

Samson & Trump, Part II
Sunday March 12, 2017

Alas, after Samson judged Israel for 20 years, he fell in with the Philistine woman, Delilah, who enticed him to give away the secret of his strength. Samson confessed to her, *"There hath not come a razor upon mine head; for I have been a Nazarite unto God from my mother's womb: If I be shaven, then my strength will go from me, and I shall become weak, and be like another man."*

The Philistines captured Samson, gouged out his eyes, brought him down to Gaza, and shackled him in irons and put him to the work of grinding in prison. But his hair began to grow again after he had been shaven.

In truth, Samson's hair was not the source of his strength; nor was he by nature or training a muscle-bound man. Samson's stature was that of an average man; his strength was in his faith and in the power of the Spirit of God, who always came upon him when he needed supernatural power. By giving away the secret of his long hair to Delilah, he was being presumptuous, determining he could overcome the Philistines in his own strength, independently of God's Spirit.

When Delilah said, *"The Philistines be upon thee, Samson."* And he awoke out of his sleep, and said, *"I will go out as at other times before, and shake myself."* Sadly, he knew not that the LORD was departed from him.

Trump, like Samson, has hair issues, but although his hair style is unique, his strength is not in his physical attributes, nor in his wealth. How well Trump understands this, I know not. God chooses to use whom he will in order to make his power known. God chose to use the Pharaoh, when he did not know that he was being used by the God of Israel to carry out his purposes in delivering the Jews from bondage. Christian ministers, who are prophetically gifted, see the hand of God upon Trump.

Trump learned from his early mentor, Norman Vincent Peale, the power of faith, which Peale presented as *"the power of positive thinking."* His teachings were simple, First have faith in God. Next, *"Believe in yourself! Have faith in your abilities! Without a humble but reasonable confidence in your own powers you cannot be successful or happy. Never talk defeat. Use words like, hope, belief, faith, victory."*

Trump has always thought big; believed he could do anything. He started his career as *"The Little Engine that Could,"* with a million-dollar loan from his father, which is chicken feed in Manhattan. Now he is the "Big Engine that Did." He won the presidency; he will build the Great Wall of Trump; he is already delivering on jobs and is determined to return America to her former glory by deregulating the market and industry. He wants to give great men the opportunity to do mighty things, which was the America Trump grew up in.

After shaving Samson's hair in his sleep, the lords of the Philistines gathered together to offer a great sacrifice unto Dagon their god, and to rejoice: for they said, *"Our god hath delivered Samson our enemy into our hand."*

And so it seemed that they finally had him after many failed attempts. But with God things are often not as they appear.

Samson & Trump, Part III
Sunday March 12, 2017

And when the people saw Samson, they praised their god: for they said, *"Our god hath delivered into our hands our enemy, and the destroyer of our country, which slew many of us."*

And it came to pass, when their hearts were merry, that they said, *"Call for Samson, that he may make us sport."*

Trump was often made sport of by the entertainment industry, Hollywood, the press, and the Democratic Party. But all the while, God was preparing for Trump to get the last laugh.

And the Philistines called for Samson out of the prison house; and he made them a show: and they set him between the pillars.

And Samson said unto the lad that held him by the hand, *"Suffer me that I may feel the pillars whereupon the house standeth, that I may lean upon them."*

Now the house was full of men and women; and all the lords of the Philistines were there; and there were upon the roof about three thousand men and women that beheld while Samson made sport.

And Samson called unto the Lord, and said, *"O Lord God, remember me, I pray thee, and strengthen me, I pray thee, only this once, O God, that I may be at once avenged of the Philistines for my two eyes."*

And Samson took hold of the two middle pillars upon which the house stood, and on which it was borne up, of the one with his right hand, and of the other with his left.

And Samson said, *"Let me die with the Philistines."* And he bowed himself with all his might; and the house fell upon the lords, and upon all the people that were therein. So the dead which he slew at his death were more than they which he slew in his life.

Then his brethren and all the house of his father came down, and took Samson, and brought him up, and buried him in the burying place of Manoah his father. And he judged Israel twenty years.

Samson had a weakness for beautiful women, whom God used in Samson's life as an *"occasion against the Philistines: for at that time the Philistines had dominion over Israel."*

Despite Samson's moral failures, he is listed as one of the heroes of faith in Hebrews 11, *who through faith subdued kingdoms [the Philistines], wrought righteousness [justice and vengeance], obtained promises, stopped the mouth of a lion, escaped the edge of the sword, out of weakness was made strong, waxed valiant in fight, turned to flight the armies of the aliens, tortured, not accepting deliverance; that he might obtain a better resurrection: And he had a test of cruel mocking, yea, moreover of bonds and imprisonment.*

Trump has been known in the past to have a weakness for attractive women. However, unlike Samson, who was finally brought down by a pagan woman, Trump was lifted up by Melania, an immigrant model, who speaks five languages. The First Lady boldly approached the throne of grace in Melborne, Florida. She pleaded with our Father in heaven to *"deliver us from evil."*

Notwithstanding Trump's past moral failures, God has already mightily used him to shake off the Philistines in Washington, the media and Hollywood, wherever the hyenas are hunting their prey.

Trump the Lionheart as he remains humble will bring down the Philistines' palace as he pushes against the two pillars of their stronghold, the Democratic Party and their cohorts in the mainstream media.

IN WAR THERE IS NO SUBSTITUTE FOR VICTORY
Sunday March 12, 2017

In reviewing some past articles I discovered that I wrote on December 7, 2014, *"America needs another lion, like our beloved Washington to save us from our enemies both foreign and domestic. God has done it before; he may do it again. I am praying for such a man, a leader like Constantine the Great or a Charles 'The Hammer' Martel. We need victory over our enemies, then peace. We should not want peace with God's enemies without victory."*

Little did I know over two years ago, that Donald J. Trump would be the answer to my prayer. Finally, a president who believes in victory!

Donald Trump says, *"Well, I'll tell you what, I don't mind fighting, but you have got to win and number one, we don't win wars, we just fight, we just fight. It's like a big -- like you're vomiting, just fight, fight, fight. We don't win anything. I mean, if you're going to fight, you win and you get back to rebuilding the country. We don't win. It's really a terrible thing. I mean, our country used to win all the time. We don't win at all anymore."*

Thank God those days are coming to an end.

Tuesday, March 14 at 11:30 am EST

I heard O'Reilly last night justify a replacement of Obamacare with the Preamble phrase, *"promote the general welfare."* Our founders did not mean the welfare state or providing a health safety net with this language.

There was no welfare state when the Constitution was ratified. Our fathers meant that any legislation should not favor one group over another.

Wednesday, March 14 at 11:52 am EST
My health care plan is to not engage in unhealthy behaviors such as smoking, drinking, and promiscuous sex. Also, I eat a balanced diet with **Plexus**® health supplements and exercise daily. I stay away from doctors as much as possible. I figure, if I am patient, the body will heal. I have never been on a medication for over two weeks, and even that has been very rare over the last 45 years.

And most of all I trust Jesus to keep me healthy, which is my preventive medicine. My plan has served me well. As far as I know, at 74 I remain healthy and as active as ever. Oh, and I am not constantly worrying about, *"What if?"*

I don't consider it the government's responsibility to take care of me in my old age. I would be fearful of what they might want to do. Try my plan, it is very inexpensive.

A Man's Man

Wednesday, March 15 at 11:00 am EST
Rapper, Snoop Dog, made a video of him assassinating the president. Anyone who would choose to call himself *Snoop Dog* must be the lowest of the low. That this pot head pervert could be so popular speaks volumes against the savages that pay to hear his rants against women and police and whatever else he raps against.

Thursday, March 16, 2017
Cal State Fullerton

I told the students, *"Just like Obama wire-tapped Trump, God has wire-tapped you all. He is listening in on all your conversations."*

Obama denies the wiretapping of Trump.

The devil lies to these filthy dreamers (students) who defile the flesh, despise dominion and speak evil of dignities, that there is no God listening in on everything they have said in secret.

Thursday, March 16 at 11:00 pm 2017 EST

"For dogs have compassed me: the assembly of the wicked have enclosed me: they pierced my hands and my feet," Psalm 22:16.

Snoop Dog would murder President Trump and Bow Wow would pimp Mrs. Trump. The hyenas in the Democratic Party enclose the President and the jackals in the media are snipping at his feet.

Watch for Lionheart to rise and roar and have the lowly beasts frightfully run away with their tails between their legs. They just don't know who they are opposing. There has never been a Republican like the Trumpster.

Friday, March 17 at 1:01 pm EST

Thankfully, we do not have to see two frumpy feminist socialists standing together, Hillary and Merkel. Merkel needs to find a new hair dresser.

Saturday, March 18 at 1:56 pm EST

Trump is a man's man.

Trump should be the example for those of us who believe professionals should still wear suits and ties. Don't people know anymore, that clothes make the man?

Jeb Bush and other politicians tried to pull off the casual look in order to relate, but it did not work.

Hillary and Merkel look manlier than the metro-sexual males of our day. If a woman aspires to be president, she should take Queen Elizabeth or Mrs. Trump as an example of a lady-like bearing.

Trump relates to the common man, because he is not a phony. Trump is unashamedly rich and the epitome of the American Spirit.

Our man, Trump, demonstrates that anyone can make it big in the USA, if he is willing to be industrious, take initiative and be independent.

Saturday, March 18 at 5:24 pm EST

The media jackals are getting on Trump for not presenting the evidence for Obama's wiretapping. Yet, the press frequently quotes unnamed or anonymous sources to support their stories. The worst example was Watergate and the "Deep Throat" source. Woodward and Bernstein were hailed as heroes of journalism. In fact, they were irresponsible journalists.

Sunday, March 19 at 1:24 am EST

I have been reviewing my running commentary about Donald Trump through the Primaries and the General Election. There is one thing about which I was wrong. I expected in the end that the media would ease up on Trump, since he makes for a large TV audience and hot press in the newspapers. His presidency was bound to be more exciting and a bigger story than a Hillary's presidency. People catch on every word of Trump, whereas Hillary was lackluster.

I thought the media would hate to lose a big story by the defeat of Trump, which would put him back to the business world. But in truth, the media got tougher and tougher against the man.

One thing that motivates the egotistical journalists is that they each hope to become a star. No star in the political or entertainment world is brighter than Trump's. The media and Hollywood stars all pale in comparison to Trump.

Reporters hoped that one of them would be the one whose coverage shot down the brightest star and elevate him (Tapper) or her (Megyn) to the status of a Woodward or Bernstein, or that a media outlet like CNN could have the impact of the Washington Post during its glory years.

Historically, there has usually been a conflict between the Second Estate, civil authority, and the Fourth Estate, the press. The Fourth Estate wants to have as much power and respect as the Second Estate.

Sometimes the Fourth Estate aligns with the Second Estate for the purposes of power, prestige and privilege, as has been the case in election cycles for the last half century with the alliance between the mainstream media and the Democratic Party. But the press and the Democrats allied could not bring down Mr. Trump.

Thank You Russians

Tuesday, March 21 at 11:33 am EST

I want to thank Mr. Putin and any other Russians for whatever they might have done to contribute to the defeat of Hillary/Obama and the victory of President Trump.

The Russians alleged help is curious, because the Democratic Party is largely Marxist in its political philosophy. Could this be a sign that the Russians are moving away from Marxism?

Perhaps the way has been paved for the Russians to do more business with the Trump enterprises. After all, as President Calvin Coolidge said, *"The business of America is business."*

What is good for Trump is good for Making American Great Again, since Mr. Trump is a great American. I hope that the Trump enterprises flourish, while he is devoting his time and effort to the affairs of state.

I am sure his sons will carry on the family tradition of success set by Grandpa Fred and Father Donald and keep the family enterprises strong. Daughter Ivanka has her office at the White House now helping Dad govern. God bless the Trumps! I hope they become richer and richer.

Wednesday, March 22 at 4:30 am EST

In President Trump's rally in Louisville, Kentucky, he spent almost five minutes talking about Henry Clay (1777-1852), who was most responsible for passing the Tariff of 1828. Clay was an advocate of *"The American System,"* which supported high tariffs to protect American industry from foreign competition and to provide revenue for internal improvements in roads, canals, etc.

Trump campaigned in favor of tariffs on goods manufactured outside the U.S. and is a strong advocate of rebuilding America's infrastructure. Remember, there was no federal income tax in the times of Clay to finance internal improvements or any other government project.

Jackson and Clay were arch political enemies. Jackson was the strongest president of the era from Jefferson to Lincoln. Henry Clay of Kentucky, John C. Calhoun of South Carolina and Daniel Webster of Massachusetts were the leading legislators, who formed the Great Triumvirate of the first half of the 19th Century. These men were renowned for their oratorical skills. Has there been any of their like in Congress in modern times?

In the Louisville speech, Trump also referred to Andrew Jackson with whom he identifies. Trump has a portrait of Jackson hanging in the Oval office. Isn't it ironic that Obama, a Democrat, presided over Jackson's face to be taken off the front of the $20 bill and a Republican resurrects him in the Oval Office.

Clay was known as *"The Great Compromiser"* and *"The Great Pacifier"* for his ability to bring others to agreement, through his oratorical skills and appeals to common sense. Will the man who wrote *"The Art of the Deal"* succeed in bringing together factions within his own party and convince some Democrats to replace Obamacare with something better? This will be one of Trump's first great tests as a deal maker. Trump is no orator in the 19th Century sense, but he does know how to connect with the masses through common sense appeals in his rousing speeches.

Will history remember President Trump as *"the Great Deal Maker?"*

Wednesday, March 22 at 11:33 am EST

Can anyone think of an example of where Congress actually repealed a law since the 21st Amendment in 1933, which repealed the 18th Amendment of 1920?

I know there are examples where Congress repeals state laws like the Civil Rights Act. However, legislators seem unwilling to repeal laws, which Congress has previously enacted.

Congressmen are notorious drinkers so they had personal interests in repealing Prohibition. Maybe since the ACA does not cover Congressmen, they don't really have the motivation to replace it.

My position is repeal Obamacare but not replace. If government is going to be involved in healthcare, let it be at the state or local level. Of course, it is best to remind people that they are responsible for paying their own way in life or rely upon family or charity.

Get government out of the healthcare business!

Alas, government involvement was accepted in the mid-sixties. Once government gets involved in our personal lives; it is unlikely they will voluntarily get out.

TRUMP AND THE ANCIENT MARINER
Saturday, March 25, 2017

So, the Republicans did not have the votes to replace Obamacare. Trump did not seem too disappointed. He said all along it may be best politically to let Obamacare implode.

Is Obamacare mortally wounded as the President has said? Did Trump inflict the mortal blow to the Albatross with his crossbow? Is he the Ancient Mariner? Is the Albatross around his neck?

> *"Instead of the cross, the Albatross*
> *About my neck was hung."*

Does the bird still hang upon the neck the Democrats? Or is it now draping the Republicans' neck? Or are working and taxpaying Americans bearing the burden?

Are we all cursed far into the future with the longest step of Socialism since Social Security?

Are the two hundred dead sailors in the poem like the Republican Congressmen, who refused to vote for Ryan's replacement plan? Who is the wedding guest to whom the Mariner told his tale? Is it you or me?

At the end of the Rime we are told,

> *"A sadder and a wiser man*
> *He rose the morrow morn."*

Friday, March 31 at 8:30 pm EST

Martha MacCallum's program, *"The First One Hundred Days,"* had one boy and two girl commentators grading Trump. They gave him below average grades because after the Republican plan for repealing and replacing Obamacare failed, he *"needed to get back on message. He was not focused this week."*

Who are these kids? What do they know about being an executive? How many times did we hear the same refrain from the pundits during the campaign? What did any of them know about running for office?

After the primaries, they said he could get away with his lack of focus during the Primaries, but not in the general election. After he won the General Election, they are saying he can't govern by getting off message.

Trump knows what he is doing. His moves and tweets are all strategic. The pundits have been wrong about him from the beginning. They have no business grading him. The lot of them should have been fired long ago.

I will say Martha MacCallum treats Trump fairly.

Sunday, April 2 at 7:41 pm EST
"Trump has 'em right where he wants 'em."

Thursday, April 6 at 10:00 am EST
Jonah Goldberg said this same old claptrap throughout the campaign, complaining about the tweeting and Trump squandering his time by involving himself in personal disputes. It is through the tweets that Trump is able to connect directly to the American people, unfiltered by a hostile or ignorant media. Trump's constitutes don't mind the disputes; we like the fight in the man. Trump was right about the Obama administration "wiretapping."

Goldberg is correct that "Character is destiny," but he is dead wrong about Trump being his own worst enemy. Does Goldberg think he has a superior character to Trump? What does journalist Goldberg know about management? Trump has a life time experience in successful leadership at the highest levels in the business world. Trump's steadfastness of character is going to make for a great Presidency.

As for Rich Lowry referring to Trump as a populist, I do not recall Trump ever describing himself as a populist, which is a vague term anyway. If it means Trump is a man of the people, then he is a populist. Goldberg says

Trump has fallen in the polls; the polls were against him throughout the General Election, yet he won the Presidency. The people who voted for him remain firm in their support of President Trump and think he is doing a great job.

Will Goldberg ever apologize for being so wrong about Trump? Since "character is destiny," the man's stubbornness and blindness would seem to make it highly unlikely.

Friday, April 7 at 7:32 am EST
Contrary to dire predictions I read on my newsfeed, Trump's missile attack on Syria, is not going to bring about WW III

Trump Made My Day
Thursday, April 13, 2017
Purdue University
By 3pm I received the news that Trump suddenly dropped the "mother of all bombs" on ISIS in Afghanistan, vaporizing Muslims moles in their holes. I announced the good news to passing students. I thought that this might get a reaction but they seemed indifferent, just like they are indifferent to the fact that the LORD is returning in flaming fire to take vengeance to those who know not God. It was a slow afternoon on campus but, Trump had already made my day.

Friday, April 15 at 6:45 am EST

I am reading where the Washington establishment has supposedly co-opted the President. But you can't tame a lion! You watch. Trump will end up mauling these people.

They are stroking him, but as my friend, Dianne Sloan, says, *"You can't pet a lion."* There are many cases where lions have ended up attacking their trainers.

Trump is always waiting to pounce at the right moment.

What is really happening is that the establishment, including both neo-cons and liberals, is getting on the Trump Train, and they are claiming it was their idea all of the time. They don't want to be completely left behind.

How many of them actually would have the let the missiles fly to Syria or dropped the *"mother of all bombs"* on ISIS? They might have talked about it. But would they have done it? Trump's military is being allowed to fight the way the generals know best and not to be restrained by politicians on the National Security Council or in the Department of Defense. Maybe it's time to call it the Department of War again.

Unfortunately, there are people who voted for Trump who do not really understand the man. They jumped on the Trump Train at the last moment because it was really the only one bound for Washington. Trump had already derailed all other Republican trains and Hillary's engine was doomed to crash as soon at the Trump Express got on the rails.

CONLUSION: THE VISION

We have embarked on the Era of Trump, where profit is no longer a dirty word. America will be rebuilt bigger and better than ever. Business will flourish and civil government will diminish. The business of America will be business again. The focus will be on success not failure. Rugged individuals will enjoy the fruit of their own labor, instead of personal profits being forcibly redistributed by the state. Homeless people will once again be considered vagrants. Immigrants will enrich this country as of old by embracing the American Dream, not the American dole. We will have a country of freemen, not serfs.

Benjamin Franklin reminded us, *"The Constitution only guarantees the American people the right to pursue happiness. You have to catch it yourself."* Donald J. Trump is the very definition of the man who caught the American Dream and the epitome of the American success story.

Let us grasp a new Golden Age for America, where captains of industry, like Trump, are allowed to flourish. May we have a country where those who supply the best product for the cheapest price are the winners, where men aspire to become employers instead of employees.

In the midst of such economic prosperity may the Church of Jesus Christ flourish and triumph. As the President labors to Make America Great Again, let the ministers of the gospel toil to make the church strong again. May she once again build majestic cathedrals, which are the most imposing, yet welcoming, structures in our grand cities. May Christians no longer wait to be raptured out of this world but occupy until the Lord returns. The church, not the state, should take on the responsibility of providing medical and educational services to the unfortunate. May churches be full on Sunday and the sports arenas closed for lack of interest.

Truth and free thinking must again prevail and political correctness will be but a bad memory. Capitalism will be triumphant and socialism will be buried. May the emphasis be no longer upon the Great Society but upon strong families, which pray together and stay together. A nation can only be great which is built on a dual foundation of strong families and an aggressive church.

May there be a revival of Christendom throughout the world through a renewed time when America unashamedly sends missionaries to convert the nations.

Donald J. Trump says, *"I like thinking big. If you're going to be thinking anything, you might as well think big."* God's people perish for a lack of vision. We experienced much of this dream in America's glory days. I remember aspects of it, which still remained in my youth.

May January 20, 2017, be regarded as the beginning new epoch in the history of America and of the world.

Thank you, Mr. President for daring to do what no other candidate in my lifetime would do, stand up to the establishment and say, *The Emperor has no clothes. Our system is bankrupt!*

Thank you for pledging your life, fortune and sacred honor to *Make America Great Again.*

Appendix A

Literally but not Seriously

By Pastor David Coke

"For My flesh is true food, and My blood is true drink. He who eats My flesh and drinks My blood abides in Me, and I in him." As a result of this many of His disciples withdrew and were not walking with Him anymore. So Jesus said to the twelve, "You do not want to go away also, do you?" Simon Peter answered Him, "Lord, to whom shall we go? You have words of eternal life. We have believed and have come to know that You are the Holy One of God." (John 6:55-56; 6:66-69)

During the recent political campaign for the Presidency, a journalist made a very astute observation concerning Donald Trump's comments and rhetoric. She opined that Mr. Trump's supporters understood his comments seriously but not literally, but his opponents understood his comments literally but not seriously. We might call this the 'liberal' gap, that bottomless chasm between socialist lies and capitalist truth or in Biblical terms, the 'great gulf fixed' so those in socialist torment (where all men are equally slaves to the state and sin, i.e. political hell on earth) cannot come to capitalist paradise (where all men are free to 'be all that you can be' and live by the dictates of conscience, i.e. political heaven on earth).

This is not some 'new' revelation or 'modern' phenomenon, it is the way men and women of truth have always been treated and until Jesus returns to destroy these God-haters, will always be treated. The fork tongued socialist promotes any comment or rhetoric about personal freedom and possibilities for one person, to mean the loss of freedom and possibilities for another person. These hypocritical elitists promote the 'zero sum game', that the rich are only rich, by making someone poor. This lie foments class envy and warfare, so these demagogues obtain power by displacing the power to break out of poverty and replacing it with hatred, violence and slavery to the state. So, what analogy can be drawn between the modern political purveyors of petty and peevish pandering (the demon-cratic party) and the ancient spiritual sowers of salacious and sanctimonious selfishness (the Phari-see(me)s)?

The Pharisees of Jesus' times are analogous to lying left-wing liberals of our day, in that they both seek power over people to control them, rather than seek to empower people to control themselves. When Jesus raised Lazarus from the dead, the Pharisees (also called 'Jews') had an emergency meeting and, in a panic, concluded that Jesus and Lazarus must die. They made this decision so they could keep their power over the people, because this miracle legitimized Jesus' preaching, *'if the Son shall set you free, you shall be free indeed'*, which would mean an END of their power and position over the people of God.

"Therefore the chief priests and the Pharisees convened a council, and were saying, 'What are we doing? For this man is performing many signs. If we let Him go on like this, all men will believe in Him, and the Romans will come and take away both our place and our nation.'"

But one of them, Caiaphas, who was high priest that year, said to them, 'You know nothing at all, nor do you take into account that it is expedient for you that one man die for the people, and that the whole nation not perish.' Now he did not say this on his own initiative, but being high priest that year, he prophesied that Jesus was going to die for the nation, and not for the nation only, but in order that He might also gather together into one the children of God who are scattered abroad. So from that day on they planned together to kill Him.' (Joh 11:47-53)

"The large crowd of the Jews then learned that He (Jesus) was there; and they came, not for Jesus' sake only, but that they might also see Lazarus, whom He raised from the dead. But the chief priests planned to put Lazarus to death also; because on account of him many of the Jews were going away and were believing in Jesus."(Joh 12:9-11)

Like Donald Trump, Jesus was taken seriously, but not literally by his disciples and taken literally but not seriously but His opponents. The majority of the Council, which consisted of the Priests, Pharisees, Sadducees and Scribes, hated Jesus and like the liberals who misunderstand Trump, they misunderstood Jesus. Following is an example:

"The Passover of the Jews was near, and Jesus went up to Jerusalem. And He found in the temple those who were selling oxen and sheep and doves, and the money changers seated at their tables. And He made a scourge of cords, and drove them all out of the temple, with the sheep and the oxen; and He poured out the coins of the money changers and overturned their tables; and to those who were selling the doves He said, 'Take these things away; stop making My Father's house a place of business.' His disciples remembered that it was written, 'ZEAL FOR YOUR HOUSE WILL CONSUME ME.'

The Jews then said to Him, 'What sign do You show us as your authority for doing these things?' Jesus answered them, 'Destroy this temple, and in three days I will raise it up.'

The Jews then said, 'It took forty-six years to build this temple, and will You raise it up in three days?' But He was speaking of the temple of His body. So when He was raised from the dead, His disciples remembered that He said this; and they believed the Scripture and the word which Jesus had spoken," (Joh 2:13-22).

After purging the Temple of worldly business to do God's business, the Pharisees took Jesus literally but not seriously, when He said *"Destroy this temple, and in three days I will raise it up,"* and they considered Him insane, *"Many of them were saying, 'He has a demon and is insane. Why do you listen to Him?'"* (Joh 10:20).

Donald Trump, like Jesus, is trying to purge the 'temple' of the United States of America, by driving the 'money changers and thieves' out of our government. He has taken a political 'whip' to the back of these corrupt 'leaders' and exposed their hypocrisy and 'turned over their tables' and intends to 'strip them naked' of power that our government might, once more, be a place to empower the people of this country to Make America Great Again.

Mr. Trump intends to 'destroy' this 'temple of doom' which is full of special interests, lobbyists and foreigners, attempting to 'pay to play', and 'raise it up again' over the next eight years by responsible, humble leadership. For this 'destroying of the temple', Mr. Trump is faced with similar opposition. His opponents consider him, like Jesus, INSANE, because if he is allowed to succeed,

202 · JED SMOCK

he will take their power from them and return it to the people. Many of the establishment 'Pharisees' and liberal hate mongers are calling for Mr. Trump's assassination or impeachment, and no doubt, as with Jesus, there are plans being made in the dark halls of political power to carry out these plans.

What might we, followers of Jesus in HOLINESS, expect from those who love their sin? Like Jesus and Mr. Trump, we will be taken literally but not seriously by our opponents and considered INSANE.

Here is an example from my own life. Some years ago, I left work mid-morning to pick-up a large order of donuts for our employees' morning coffee break. As I approached the cashier to pay, she asked, "How are you today?"; to which I replied, "I'm obeying God, I can't do better than that!"

She thought for a moment and inquired, "Do you mean you don't sin?" She had the obvious meaning "YOU CAN'T BE SERIOUS! EVERYBODY SINS." She took me literally but not seriously and looked at me like I was INSANE.

The Apostle Peter warns,

> "Beloved, do not be surprised at the fiery ordeal among you, which comes upon you for your testing, as though some strange thing were happening to you; but to the degree that you share the sufferings of Christ, keep on rejoicing, so that also at the revelation of His glory you may rejoice with exultation. If you are reviled for the name of Christ, you are blessed, because the Spirit of glory and of God rests on you... but if anyone suffers as a Christian, he is not to be ashamed, but is to glorify God in this name. For it is time for

judgment to begin with the household of God; and if it begins with us first, what will be the outcome for those who do not obey the gospel of God? AND IF IT IS WITH DIFFICULTY THAT THE RIGHTEOUS IS SAVED, WHAT WILL BECOME OF THE GODLESS MAN AND THE SINNER? (1Pe 4:12-18).

All of us, who believe the Bible when it says that the standard for approval before God is HOLINESS, will suffer the same fate of Jesus and Mr. Trump, we will be taken literally but not seriously and for this, we will be hated.

John writes,

"Beloved, now we are children of God, and it has not appeared as yet what we will be. We know that when He appears, we will be like Him, because we will see Him just as He is. And everyone who has this hope fixed on Him purifies himself, just as He is pure. Everyone who practices sin also practices lawlessness; and sin is lawlessness. You know that He appeared in order to take away sins; and in Him there is no sin. No one who abides in Him sins; no one who sins has seen Him or knows Him. Little children, make sure no one deceives you; the one who practices righteousness is righteous, just as He is righteous; the one who practices sin is of the devil; for the devil has sinned from the beginning. The Son of God appeared for this purpose, to destroy the works of the devil. No one who is born of God practices sin, because His seed abides in him; and he cannot sin, because he is born of God. By this the children of God and the children of the devil are obvious: anyone who does

not practice righteousness is not of God, nor the one who does not love his brother. For this is the message which you have heard from the beginning, that we should love one another; not as Cain, who was of the evil one and slew his brother. And for what reason did he slay him? Because his deeds were evil, and his brother's were righteous. Do not be surprised, brethren, if the world hates you," (1Jn 3:2-13).

APPENDIX B
Frederick T. Gelder

My maternal grandfather, Frederick T. Gelder (1874-1955), was editor and publisher of the Forest City News in Pennsylvania from 1898 to 1955. He wrote weekly column, JUST A WORD IN PASSING over a period of 52 years.

From 1924 to 1940, he was Republican Senator from the 23rd District to the Pennsylvania Senate. During his last term, he was elected President Pro-Tempore of the Senate.

The following are excerpts from his column:

JUST A WORD IN PASSING, February 11, 1954: Perhaps the infiltration of government into our lives—even in attempts at helpfulness has sapped from us some of the fortitude, independence and self-reliance of the pioneers.

We have reached the point where we do not just hope, we demand, that the government comes to the rescue on any and all occasions. We've wandered far astray from the viewpoint of former president Grover Cleveland, who is 1887 enunciated the principle that 'though the people support the government, the Government should not support the people.'

It is said that one out of every eight persons in the country is receiving Federal money in one form or another. There isn't a chance that the country will ever get back to the fundamental proclaimed by that robust Democratic president, but it is well to remember that each and every time the government helps one group it does so only with money it takes from other groups.

JUST A WORD IN PASSING, March 18,1954: Said Andrew Carnegie: 'Take away my fortune, destroy my plants, but leave me my key men and I will build everything again.' Guess it was Elbert Hubbard who put it: 'A business is the lengthened shadow of a man.' He also suggested: 'Responsibilities gravitate to the shoulders that can bear them.' Probably both men had the same thing in mind—the importance and value of the man who get things done. Eisenhower has a colossal job. He's doing well. Let's stand behind him.'"

JUST A WORD IN PASSING, August 26, 1954, Time was, in the good old days of the past, when every mother told her young hopeful he might be president someday, that the young Horatio Alger readers visualized a time when they too might be rich—at least quite prosperous. Today the idea seems to be to cut everybody down to the average size.

Yet it was the exceptional man, rather than the so-called common man, who made America what it is today. As Herbert Hoover said on his 80th birthday, 'There is no such thing as the common man, for each of us can be sure that he possesses his own qualities and distinction.' As he says this common man appellation 'is the negation of individual dignity and a slogan of mediocrity and uniformity.'

Other Titles by Bro. Jed Smock

Who Will Rise Up? *An Autobiographical Classic on Open-air Evangelism.*

Grieve Not the Spirit, *A Treatise on Sin, Righteousness and Judgment.*

Walking in the Spirit, *A Liberating Commentary of Romans 6, 7, & 8.*

Christ Triumphant, *The Battle of the Ages.*

The Mystery of Christ Revealed: *The Key to Understanding Predestination.*

Website: brojed.org
Email: brojed@aol.com
cindysmock@aol.com
Facebook: Jed Smock (Brother Jed)
YouTube: Brother Jed Channel
Phone 573-999-0347   573-999-0346

Address:
Brother Jed Smock
The Campus Ministry USA
PO Box 3845
Terre Haute, IN 47803

Bro. Jed wearing his Trump button.

Brother Jed, center in the black coat, preaching at Texas A&M University Feb. 2016.

If you would like to help CMUSA continue to reach college students with this Gospel of Jesus Christ, you may send a gift to the above address or give on our website, brojed.org. Thank you and pray for us. **Bro. Jed**

Made in the USA
San Bernardino, CA
14 February 2018